ANGELA'S ASHES

Frank McCourt

TECHNICAL DIRECTOR Maxwell Krohn
EDITORIAL DIRECTOR Justin Kestler
MANAGING EDITOR Ben Florman

SERIES EDITORS Boomie Aglietti, Justin Kestler
PRODUCTION Christian Lorentzen

WRITER Catherine Buchanan
EDITORS Emma Chastain, Justin Kestler

This edition published by Spark Publishing

Spark Publishing
A Division of SparkNotes LLC
120 Fifth Avenue, 8th Floor
New York, NY 10011

02 03 04 05 SN 9 8 7 6 5 4 3 2 1

Please send all comments and questions or report errors to
feedback@sparknotes.com.

Library of Congress information available upon request

Printed and bound in the United States

RRD-C

ISBN 1-58663-469-0

INTRODUCTION: STOPPING TO BUY SPARKNOTES ON A SNOWY EVENING

Whose words these are you *think* you know.
Your paper's due tomorrow, though;
We're glad to see you stopping here
To get some help before you go.

Lost your course? You'll find it here.
Face tests and essays without fear.
Between the words, good grades at stake:
Get great results throughout the year.

Once school bells caused your heart to quake
As teachers circled each mistake.
Use SparkNotes and no longer weep,
Ace every single test you take.

Yes, books are lovely, dark, and deep,
But only what you grasp you keep,
With hours to go before you sleep,
With hours to go before you sleep.

Contents

CONTEXT

FRANK MCCOURT SPENT HIS INFANT YEARS in Brooklyn, his impoverished adolescence in Limerick, Ireland, and most of his adult life as a teacher in the United States. Though he never attended high school, McCourt spent more than thirty years teaching writing at Stuyvesant, a prestigious public high school in New York City. McCourt found his teaching career—which he has referred to as a "learning career"—fulfilling, but he never gave up his dream of becoming a writer. When he retired from teaching, McCourt and his brother Malachy began to perform a two-man show entitled *A Couple of Blackguards,* which featured many of the songs the McCourts sang together back in Ireland.

McCourt decided to pursue his dream of becoming a writer by telling his own story, in the present tense, more than four decades after he left behind Ireland and the bleak, painful upbringing that fills his memoir. Waiting decades before writing his autobiography gave McCourt the perspective to talk about his troubled childhood at a comfortable distance. He treats the subject of his own difficult life with evenhandedness and objectivity, showing none of the spite, regret, or rancor we might expect. Yet he never downplays the suffering from acute hunger and deprivation he endured throughout his youth. As he has said, *Angela's Ashes* is "an epic of woe."

Angela's Ashes won the Pulitzer Prize, the National Book Critics' Circle Award, and spent 117 weeks on *The New York Times* hardcover best-seller list. McCourt's memoir and its sequel, *'Tis,* which tells of his experiences as a young man in America, have become worldwide best-sellers translated into many languages. A film version of *Angela's Ashes* appeared in 1999. Both books have vaulted McCourt from an unknown first-time writer in his late sixties to a world-renowned author deluged with thousands of fan letters and requests for speaking engagements. McCourt's success is a testament to patience and perseverance. *Angela's Ashes* serves as a living record of the strong moral values and healthy sense of humor McCourt maintained despite the suffering and woe he endured as a child.

PLOT OVERVIEW

T HE NARRATOR, FRANK MCCOURT, describes how his parents meet in Brooklyn, New York. After his mother, Angela, becomes pregnant with Frank, she marries Malachy, the father of her child. Angela struggles to feed her growing family of sons, while Malachy spends his wages on alcohol. Frank's much-loved baby sister, Margaret, dies and Angela falls into depression. The McCourts decide to return to Ireland. More troubles plague the McCourts in Ireland: Angela has a miscarriage, Frank's two younger brothers die, and Malachy continues to drink away the family's money.

Frank's childhood is described as a time of great deprivation, but of good humor and adventure as well. When the first floor of the house floods during the winter, Angela and Malachy announce that the family will leave the cold damp of the first floor, which they call "Ireland," and move to the warm, cozy second floor, which they call "Italy." Although Malachy's alcoholism uses up all of the money for food, he earns Frank's love and affection by entertaining him with stories about Irish heroes and the people who live on their lane.

Over the course of a few years, Angela gives birth to two sons, Michael and Alphonsus. Alphosus is called "Alphie" for short. As Frank grows older, the narration increasingly focuses on his exploits at school. When Frank turns ten, he is confirmed (Confirmation is a ritual that makes one an official Christian or Catholic. When Frank was growing up, people were confirmed around ages seven to ten). Right after his confirmation, Frank falls ill with typhoid fever and must stay in the hospital for months. There, he gets his first introduction to Shakespeare. Frank finds comfort in stories of all kinds, from Shakespeare to movies to newspapers. By the time he returns to school, his gift for language is obvious. In particular, Frank's flair for storytelling gets him noticed by his teacher.

With the onset of World War II, many fathers in Limerick go to England to find work and send money back to their families. Eventually, Malachy goes as well, but he fails to send money home. Frank begins to work for Mr. Hannon. This is the first in a series of jobs. Frank will go on to work for Mr. Timoney, Uncle Ab, the post office, Mrs. Finucane, and Mr. McCaffrey. Frank enjoys the feeling of

PLOT OVERVIEW

responsibility he gets from working, and he dreams of saving enough to provide his family with food and clothes.

The McCourts get evicted from their lodgings and must move in with Angela's cousin Laman. Angela begins sleeping with Laman, an arrangement that makes Frank increasingly uncomfortable and angry. He also begins to feel guilty about his own sexual feelings. The priests' strict mandates against masturbation make Frank feel guilty when he masturbates.

While working as a messenger boy, Frank begins a sexual relationship with a customer, Theresa Carmody, who eventually dies of consumption, leaving Frank heartbroken. Frank saves enough money to get to New York. On his first night there, he attends a party and sleeps with an American woman. Though sad to leave behind Ireland and his family, Frank has great expectations for the future.

CHARACTER LIST

Frank McCourt The book's author, narrator, and protagonist. As the teller of his own life story, McCourt writes from the perspective of an adolescent looking out onto the world rather than as an adult looking back on his childhood. McCourt's memoir therefore maintains a voice and perspective rich with the enthusiasm, tenderness, and determination of a young man.

Angela McCourt Frank's "Mam" is humorous and loving, not overbearing or self-pitying, despite her difficult life. As Angela deals with her husband's alcoholism, the deaths of three of her children, and the necessity of begging for handouts from aid agencies, her expectations disintegrate. Despite the painful thwarting of her own hopes, Angela always considers her children and their welfare above all else.

Malachy McCourt (Sr.) Malachy is an alcoholic who spends his wages and dole money on drink while his children starve. McCourt's treatment of his father remains masterfully evenhanded. He reveals not only the despair inflicted on the family by Malachy's drinking, but also the obvious love between Malachy and his sons.

Malachy McCourt (Jr.) Frank's younger brother by one year. Malachy is named after his father. He is more physically attractive than Frank, and manages to charm his way into the hearts of cantankerous people.

Oliver and Eugene McCourt Frank's younger twin brothers. They die within several months of one another, shortly after the McCourts arrive in Limerick. Their deaths devastate Angela, who is already grieving over the loss of her baby girl, Margaret.

Michael McCourt Frank's second youngest brother, born in Limerick, whom Frank believes was left by an angel on the seventh step of their house.

Alphie McCourt Frank's youngest brother.

Aunt Aggie Angela's sister and Frank's miserly aunt. Aunt Aggie initially resents the McCourt children. Although she never ceases to be rude and unpleasant, she proves her loyalty to the family by helping them through tough times.

Pa Keating Frank's warm and caring uncle. Pa Keating bolsters Frank's confidence and encourages him to follow his own instincts in adulthood.

Ab Sheehan Angela's brother and Frank's uncle. Uncle Ab was dropped on his head as a child, which damaged his brain. Frank moves in with Ab when he fights with his mother and Laman Griffin.

Grandma Grandma helps the McCourts whenever she can, although she remains suspicious of Malachy Sr.'s northern Irish roots and insists that Frank has inherited his father's "odd manner."

Laman Griffin Angela's cousin and lover for a short time. Frank has a fight with Laman that causes Frank to move in with his Uncle Ab.

The MacNamara sisters Angela's cousins who live in New York. The MacNamara sisters are bossy, burly women who keep their husbands in check and interfere in everyone else's business.

Mr. Timoney An old eccentric to whom Frank reads Jonathan Swift's satirical essay "A Modest Proposal." Mr. Timoney becomes a close friend of Frank's, in part because he respects Frank and treats him like an adult.

Theresa Carmody A seventeen-year-old consumptive girl with whom Frank has a sexual relationship. Frank desperately worries about the fate of Theresa's immortal soul, which he thinks he is jeopardizing by having premarital sex with her.

The Hannons Bridey Hannon is Angela's neighbor in Roden Lane and her favorite confidante. Bridey gives her friend much-needed support and empathy. Bridey's father is Mr. Hannon, whom Frank grows to love like a father after the old man gives him his first job delivering coal.

Patricia Madigan A young diphtheria patient whom Frank meets in the hospital while he is recovering from typhoid. Patricia reads poems to Frank and jokes with him.

Seamus The hospital janitor who helps Frank and Patricia communicate, and who later recites poetry to Frank in the eye hospital.

Mrs. Brigid Finucane The old woman to whose debtors Frank writes threatening letters.

Mr. McCaffrey Frank's boss at Easons, Ltd., a company that imports and distributes Protestant newspapers from Northern Ireland.

The Molloys Mikey Molloy is Frank's cross-eyed school friend who has fits and is an expert on sex-related topics. Mikey's father, Peter, is famous as the champion pint drinker of Limerick, while his mother, Nora, is well-known for her frequent visits to the insane asylum. Like Angela, Nora worries about how she will feed her family when her husband drinks away all his money.

Billy Campbell Another friend of Frank's who shares many adventures with him.

Paddy Clohessy A school friend of Frank's who lives in unbearable squalor as a child, but who eventually moves to England in order to earn more money for his family.

Mr. O'Halloran Frank's headmaster and teacher during his final year at school. "Hoppy" encourages Frank to go to America and find good employment rather than stay in a dead-end job in Ireland.

Peter Dooley Frank's hunchbacked friend who wants to work for the BBC as a radio newsreader.

ANALYSIS OF MAJOR CHARACTERS

FRANK MCCOURT

McCourt writes his memoir in the present tense from the perspective of a young boy. The memoir often distances Frank, the young boy who simply reports on events without forming opinions, from McCourt, who offers the reader a deeper, more adult perspective on those events. Frank is lively and streetwise, thoughtful and sensitive. Though physically weak and prone to infection, he has emotional strength and a survivor mentality. He is also a highly intelligent, diligent student and a quick thinker.

As the narrative progresses, Frank strives to reach beyond the limitations forced upon him by poverty. He becomes determined to achieve success in life and to provide for his family and, indeed, he is relieved to leave school at age fourteen in order to get a job. Though he does not explicitly acknowledge it, Frank is burdened by the necessity of acting as a father figure for his family.

As Frank matures, he starts to suffer from an overwhelming sense of guilt. He worries that by sinning he has doomed himself and the people he loves. Frank channels the disappointments of his difficult life into self-recrimination. Frank escapes his fears and guilt by reading, watching movies, listening to the radio, and daydreaming. He also thinks optimistically about the future, gradually focusing not just on what he wants to do for his family, but on what he wants to achieve for himself. Frank reconciles himself to the fact that in order to reach America, he will have to take risks, pass up safe jobs, and perform ethically dubious tasks such as writing threatening letters for Mrs. Finucane and delivering Protestant newspapers.

ANGELA MCCOURT

Despite constant poverty, a criminally irresponsible husband, and the death of three of her children, Angela is a loving mother who retains her sense of humor. Angela must sacrifice her standards of dignity and class in order to provide for her children. Still, she never lowers her expectations for her sons—she raises them to be well-behaved, conscientious, kind, and hardworking men.

Frank often reacts harshly to the measures Angela takes to help her family, condemning her for begging outside a church and later for sleeping with Laman Griffin. However, despite Frank's hostility to some of her decisions, it is clear that Angela is simply struggling to cope under highly difficult and painful circumstances. McCourt makes it clear that Angela's first priority is her sons' welfare.

MALACHY MCCOURT (SR.)

In some ways, Frank's father can be considered the antagonist of *Angela's Ashes,* because his actions keep the McCourts destitute. (As antagonist is a character or obstacle in a literary work that opposes the protagonist and causes the major conflict.) While his family suffers from crippling hunger, and his children contract diseases caused by weakness and malnutrition, Malachy drinks excessively and comes home roaring that his sons must be ready to die for Ireland.

Frank's father drinks himself into a stupor partially to dull the pain of the deaths of his twin sons and baby daughter. But McCourt emphasizes that Malachy's drinking is more than just a means of coping with bereavement; it is an illness that constantly jeopardizes the survival of his family. Despite the burdens that Malachy's alcoholism places on Frank's shoulders, Frank almost always remains loyal to his father. He treasures the times that he and Malachy sit chatting and drinking tea in front of the fire and loves his father's way with words, his lively imagination, and his flair for storytelling.

When Malachy goes to work in England, he uses his physical distance to justify abandoning his family, leaving them without his emotional or financial support.

THEMES, MOTIFS & SYMBOLS

THEMES

Themes are the fundamental and often universal ideas explored in a literary work.

THE LIMITATIONS IMPOSED BY CLASS

Because of social snobbery, Frank is unfairly denied many opportunities. Although he is an intelligent, quick-witted, and eager student, he is prevented from becoming an altar boy and deprived of chances to further his education, because when people see him dressed in rags, they shun him. Frank's natural fighting instincts and the encouragement of a few family members help him to oppose and overcome the limits set by his low-class status.

Even small victories, such as beating a team of wealthy boys in a soccer game, help to bolster Frank's self-esteem. As the memoir progresses, Frank grows determined to prove that he can succeed and earn people's respect. In particular, he looks to America as a classless society where his ambitions will be realized and his talents rewarded, despite his lower-class upbringing. Some might view Frank's vision of America a classless society as idealistic, since class consciousness pervades American society as well. Even so, McCourt's success as a teacher, performer, and world-renowned author stands as a testament to his ability to surmount the impediments of class, and to the society that made his idealistic dream a reality beyond his—or anyone's—greatest expectations.

HUNGER

Frank is plagued by hunger throughout his childhood. The McCourts never have enough food to eat, and the food they do manage to procure is scant and unsatisfying. Hunger is mentioned over and over again until it becomes a haunting presence in the narrative. Frank's father often drinks away the money the family needs for food, and comes home wailing about the plight of Ireland and the Irish. Frank's mother realizes the pettiness of patriotism compared to the very real hunger her children suffer on a daily basis. When her husband sings songs about "suffering Ireland," she responds, "Ireland can kiss [my] arse." Frank then observes, "[F]ood on the table is what she wants, not suffering Ireland."

Food assumes a symbolic as well as a practical value in the memoir. Frank starts to associate feeling satiated with feeling like an independent and successful member of society. Frank's need for food is thus more than physical: he craves the self-esteem and freedom that come with being able to eat what he wants. Frank is unwilling to appear needy or to appeal to other people's charitable instincts to satisfy his hunger. In fact, he would rather steal than beg to survive. Once, when Malachy brings home a week's pay, Frank notices how his mother can again hold her head up in the grocery and pay the man behind the counter. "There's nothing worse in the world," he muses, "than to owe and be beholden to anyone." Here once more we see how the ability to pay for one's food brings dignity and self-respect.

MOTIFS

Motifs are recurring structures, contrasts, or literary devices that can help to develop and inform the text's major themes.

ANTI-ENGLISH SENTIMENT

In the opening lines of his memoir, McCourt ascribes some of the sorrow he endured as a child to "the English and the terrible things they did to us for eight hundred long years." Most of the adult characters in the memoir condemn past English invasions of Ireland and contemporary English repression of the Irish. Frank is brought up assuming that the English are essentially immoral and evil. He is taught from the start that Ireland thrived before the English came and spoiled their way of life. Once, when his father is outside trying to beat the fleas out of a mattress, a passerby watches and says that there were no fleas in "ancient Ireland"—the English brought them over to drive the Irish "out of our wits entirely." "I wouldn't put it past the English," he adds. A revealing turn occurs when Frank hears Mr. O'Halloran say that the Irish, as well as the English, committed atrocities in battle. From this point on, Frank starts to question the assumption that Irishmen versus Englishmen means good versus evil.

STORIES, SONGS, AND FOLKTALES

As a young child, Frank loves listening to his father's boundless repertoire of stories and folktales. Often Malachy returns from the bar drunk and gregarious, telling stories of the lives of great Irish heroes, or of neighbors who live down the lane. Song has a important place in Irish culture, and bits and pieces of rhymes from old tunes pervade *Angela's Ashes*. Most of the songs tell of better days gone by and express regret at joy remembered in times of grave suffering. Lines like "Oh, for one of those hours of gladness, gone, alas, like our youth too soon" resound throughout the memoir. Frank later finds comfort in hearing Shakespeare, P. D. Wodehouse, and songs and poems read aloud by his friends and family.

GUILT

Throughout his childhood, Frank is burdened by guilt at his own sinfulness, particularly the sinfulness of his sexual thoughts and behavior. He frequently worries that he is damned or that he has damned other people. McCourt suggests that his guilt results primarily from his Catholicism. In the days of Frank's childhood, priests tirelessly cautioned against the evils of masturbation and sex—their admonishments haunt Frank's thoughts. As he matures, Frank learns to use Confession to relieve himself of guilt, and he stops feeling doomed by his natural sexual impulses.

SYMBOLS

Symbols are objects, characters, figures, or colors used to represent abstract ideas or concepts.

THE RIVER SHANNON

The symbolism of the River Shannon changes as Frank's outlook matures during his childhood and adolescence. Initially, the river symbolizes Limerick's bleakness and the brooding desolation of Frank's childhood. Frank associates the river with the endless rain that torments Limerick, which he describes as a virulent disease-carrying wetness that causes people to fall sick with coughs, asthma, consumption, and other diseases. As the memoir progresses, Frank begins to see the river as a route out of Limerick. As a result, it comes to symbolize escape, movement, and freedom. When Frank throws Mrs. Finucane's ledger into the river—thus liberating all of her remaining debtors—he suggests that soon he, like the ledger, will use the river to leave Ireland behind and set sail across the Atlantic.

ASHES

Angela's Ashes takes its name from the ashes which fall from Angela's cigarettes and those in the fireplace at which she stares blankly. The entire setting of the narrative feels draped in ash— dark, decrepit, weak, lifeless, sunless. Angela's ashes represent her crumbling hopes: her dreams of raising a healthy family with a supportive husband have withered and collapsed, leaving her with only cigarettes for comfort and the smoldering ashes of a fire for warmth.

EGGS

Unlike other families, the McCourts cannot afford to buy eggs regularly. Eggs are a familiar yet unattainable luxury, and Frank associates them with wealth and security. They become symbols of the good life that Frank wishes to provide for himself and his family. Eggs symbolize the financial security, the satisfaction, and the indulgences available beyond the boundaries of Limerick.

SYMBOLS

Summary & Analysis

Chapter I

It was, of course, a miserable childhood: the happy childhood is hardly worth your while. Worse than the ordinary miserable childhood is the miserable Irish childhood, and worse yet is the miserable Irish Catholic childhood.   (See QUOTATIONS, p. 53)

SUMMARY

As *Angela's Ashes* opens, Frank describes how his parents meet and marry in New York, then eventually move back to Ireland with their four sons. He characterizes his upbringing as a typical "miserable Irish Catholic childhood," complete with a drunken father and a downtrodden, browbeaten mother. He tells of Limerick's interminable rain, which spreads disease throughout the town.

Frank then backtracks and tells the story of his mother and father's lives before the birth of their children. Malachy McCourt, Frank's father, grows up in the north of Ireland, fights for the Old IRA, and commits a crime (unspecified by the narrator) for which a price is placed on his head. Malachy escapes to America to avoid being killed. After indulging his drinking habit in the States and in England for many years, he returns to Belfast, where he drinks tea and waits to die.

Angela Sheehan, Frank's mother, grows up in a Limerick slum. She is named after the Angelus (midnight bells rung to honor the New Year), because she was born as the bells rang. Her father drops her baby brother on his head and runs off to Australia. Ab Sheehan, Angela's brother, is never the same after being dropped, but Frank recalls that all of Limerick loved him.

Angela later emigrates to America, where she meets Malachy, who had just served three months in jail for the theft of a truck carrying buttons. Angela becomes pregnant by Malachy. Angela's cousins, the McNamara sisters, coerce Malachy into marrying Angela. He plots to escape the marriage by moving to California, but he foils his own plot by spending his train fare at the pub. The McNamara sisters mock Malachy for his strange ways and intimate that he has a "streak of the Presbyterian" in him. Frank is born and baptized, and is joined a year later by a brother, Malachy. A couple of years later, Angela gives birth to twin boys, Eugene and Oliver.

The rest of the chapter describes the difficulties and the joys of Frank's early childhood in New York. Frank remembers playing with Malachy in the park near their home, and listening to his father's patriotic songs and folk tales. He recalls particularly liking one story about a great Irish warrior named Cuchulain, and jealously guarding this story as his own. Even though Frank's father loves his children, he constantly drinks and loses jobs. He often spends his wages at the pub, and as a result Angela has no money to buy dinner for her children.

Angela has a beautiful daughter, Margaret, who inspires Malachy to stop drinking for a while, but by the end of the chapter Margaret dies. The death of her daughter drives Angela into a state of depression and causes her to neglect her children. Despite the best attempts of two of the McCourts' neighbors, Mrs. Leibowitz and Minnie McAdorey, the situation does not improve. The women decide to inform Delia and Philomena McNamara of their cousin's troubles. The McNamara sisters write to Angela's mother, asking for money to pay for the McCourts' passage back to Ireland. The chapter ends with four-year-old Frank watching as his mother vomits over the side of the ship and the Statue of Liberty recedes in the distance.

ANALYSIS

McCourt's wry humor undercuts the bleakness of his early years, as he jokes that a happy childhood "is hardly worth your while." In spite of the hardship he endured, Frank remembers the occasional happiness of his childhood in New York, playing with boys from the neighborhood and listening to his father's tales of Ireland. The introductory paragraphs of *Angela's Ashes* help to distinguish Frank, the child telling his story in the present tense, from McCourt, the grown man looking back on his life with the informed perspective of an adult.

McCourt interrupts the flow of his narrative with snippets of folk songs and old Irish tales, so that Ireland seems eternally present in the world of New York. The theme of telling tales, and the impact tales have on Frank, returns throughout the novel. The narrator comes to depend on these imaginative excursions to provide insulation from the cold realities of his life. Frank is fascinated by Freddie Leibowitz's tale of Samson, and is highly protective of his own and all the neighboring children's right to individual stories. For instance, he scolds his brother Malachy for singing a song that Frank thinks belongs to Maisie MacAdorey. Also, Frank's tale of Cuchulain unites him with his father. The narrator suggests that in a world where material possessions are scarce, ownership of songs and stories is crucial.

Malachy's alcoholism—referred to only half-jokingly as the "Curse of the Irish"—runs through this chapter. Frank recalls only one period of respite from Malachy's incessant drinking: the few weeks following Margaret's birth. The happiness of the McCourt family around this time is poignant in contrast to the despair they endure after the baby's death. Angela, until this point a gritty, loving, and responsible mother, is made miserable by the death. Food brought by kind neighbors becomes a solace to Frank in his physical and emotional state of need. However, even as he relishes Mrs. Leibowitz's soup, the boy wishes that his baby sister could be there to enjoy it too. Such details shape our reaction to Frank as much as they inform us of the events of his early childhood. Frank comes across as loving, intelligent, and deeply sensitive to the emotions of those around him.

McCourt conveys his childhood impressions of New York with sensitivity and humor, while remaining true to the language and sentiments of a four-year-old boy. For example, McCourt describes his twin brothers' diapers as "shitty" and includes all the silly jokes he can recall sharing with his brother Malachy. McCourt's word choice and humor in this introductory chapter create a tone that is both knowing and naïve.

CHAPTER II

Summary
Upon their arrival in Ireland, the McCourt family goes to Malachy's parents in County Antrim, Northern Ireland. Grandpa seems considerate of Angela, but Grandma greets her son's family coldly; Frank's aunts only nod when introduced to their brother's family. Grandma tells her son that there is no work in Ireland, and Grandpa advises him to go to the IRA and ask for money in recognition of his service.

The next morning, the family takes a bus to Dublin. Frank's father points out Lough Neagh, the lake where Cuchulain used to swim. Upon arriving in Dublin, Malachy takes Frank to the office of a man in charge of IRA pension claims. The man refuses to give the McCourts any money, saying he has no record of Malachy's service. After Malachy asks for enough money for a pint, the man refuses to give him even enough money for bus fare home. Night has fallen, and the family sleeps in a local police barracks, where the kind police and their prisoners joke with the children. The next day, the sergeant's wife tells Angela that the police have raised a collection to pay for the McCourts' train fare to Limerick. Frank's father shows Frank a statue of Cuchulain outside Dublin's General Post Office.

Frank's family receives another stony welcome when they arrive in Limerick, this time from Grandma, Angela's mother. Angela's sister, Aunt Aggie, is living with her mother because she has had a fight with her husband, Pa Keating. The next day, Grandma helps the McCourts find a furnished room on Windmill Street. The family must share one mattress, but they are grateful for it after nights of sleeping on floors. That night, however, they discover that the mattress is infested with fleas.

A few days later, Angela has a miscarriage and must go to the hospital. Malachy finds out that his dole is only nineteen shillings a week; to supplement that money, Angela goes to the St. Vincent de Paul Society for charity. Although the other women waiting for money are initially suspicious of Angela, with her American coat and Yankee children, they warm to her after she tells them of the loss of her baby. Angela receives a docket for groceries and befriends a kind, funny woman named Nora Molloy. Nora accompanies Frank's mother to the grocery store to make sure the saleswoman does not cheat Angela. The two women sit outside smoking cigarettes while Nora tells Angela about her husband, "Peter Molloy, champion pint drinker."

Soon Frank's one-year-old brother Oliver becomes ill, and his parents take him to the hospital. Grandma takes Frank and his brothers, Malachy and Eugene, to their Aunt Aggie's, where the boys eat porridge. Uncle Pa holds Malachy on his knee, a sight that makes Aggie cry, because she has no children of her own. The children return home to find that Oliver has died. At his brother's burial, Frank throws stones at the jackdaws that perch on trees all around the burial site. The next day, Frank's father spends all of his dole money on drink.

The McCourt family moves into a room on Hartstonge Street. Angela shames her husband by collecting his dole from the Labour Exchange to prevent him from drinking it away, and Frank and Malachy start school. The narrator describes Leamy's National School as a hard place where you "must not cry" if you want to earn the respect of your peers. Frank's master in the fifth class is called Mr. O' Dea, a man who can always wring tears from his students.

Tragedy again befalls the McCourts as Eugene dies of pneumonia, six months after the death of his twin brother. The doctor prescribes pills for Angela's nerves, and Frank's father copes with his grief by drinking himself into a stupor. The day Eugene dies, the adults mourn, and Pa Keating tries to distract everyone by telling funny stories. On the day of Eugene's funeral, while the dead boy is laid out in bed at home, Frank has to retrieve his father from the pub. He sees that his father has placed his pint of Guinness on top of Eugene's pristine white coffin. After the funeral, the two surviving McCourt boys eat fish and chips, and Frank thinks of Eugene and how he has been swept by angels from his cold grave and taken up to heaven to see Oliver and Margaret.

ANALYSIS

Although Angela tells the sergeant's wife that it feels good to be "back among our own," she is clearly worried about her family's future in Ireland. Just as Angela has mixed emotions about coming home, Angela and Malachy's families are not looking forward to the McCourts' return. It is clear, however, that the grandparents' restraint is not the result of unkindness but of worry. Malachy's mother does not have enough room or money to feed and house six people, and Angela's mother feels pity, anger, and anxiety over her daughter's condition: Angela has a deadbeat drunk husband, no money, and four little children.

The McCourts are strangers everywhere they go. In America, everyone sees them as Irish, and in Ireland, everyone sees them as American. Over and over people ask with varying degrees of incredulity, disgust, or interest if the boys are Yankees. Because of her American coat, Angela is initially treated coolly by the women waiting for assistance from the St. Vincent de Paul Society. When the boys at school find out that Frank grew up in New York, they taunt him and ask if he is a "gangster" or a "cowboy." The conversation results in a fistfight.

This fistfight emphasizes the contrast between the dark-haired, dark-eyed Frank and the blue-eyed, blond-ringleted Malachy. In contrast to Malachy, who is sunny and happy and beloved by all, Frank shares some of what his grandmother calls his father's northern oddities. He is introspective, and when stirred, "the blackness" comes over him.

As in America, the McCourts' first months in Limerick are filled with hardship and misfortune. Death saturates the memoir, and while always horrifyingly sad, it begins to seem almost routine. Eugene dies, and the similarity of his death and funeral to Oliver's death and funeral is striking. Death is not sentimental, romantic, or rare—it is quick, dirty, and predictable. After a tender paragraph about Malachy Sr.'s hope that his oldest sons' kindness will help Eugene forget Oliver, the next paragraph begins, "He died anyway." This bluntness is not cruel; it is a realistic portrayal of the blank suddenness of death.

The protagonist does not apportion blame for his siblings' deaths, and neither does Angela. In fact, the narrator never overtly criticizes his father, in part because the five-year-old Frankie would not have done so. Still, the image of two black pints standing on top of Eugene's white coffin seems plainly symbolic, suggesting that Malachy's alcoholism kills his children. It is surprisingly difficult to determine whether the author feels bitterness toward his father, as he only hints at his buried resentment. Frank's uncertainty about how to respond to his father's alcoholism comes through in his comment that he "didn't know what to say" to his father when Malachy spent his entire dole on drink.

McCourt encourages us to pity and understand his father. Malachy might refuse to remove his pint from its resting place on Eugene's coffin, but he is genuinely tormented by his children's deaths. He weeps for them and beats his legs in anguish. We are made to see how it is possible and even understandable that Malachy would spend money on drink while his family starves at home: after Oliver's death, Malachy takes Frank from store to store, begging for food. Malachy is turned down everywhere, mocked for coming from the North, and he is told he should be ashamed of himself. When someone kindly offers him a pint, we observe how drinking with friends mitigates the humiliation and desperation Malachy endures.

McCourt also shows us how Irish culture encourages drinking. People think of drink as medicine, as a symbol of friendship, as "the staff of life," as Pa Keating says. Malachy is helplessly dependent on alcohol, and his friends and family often inadvertently encourage his dependence. For example, when Malachy wants to get a drink after Eugene dies and Angela objects, Grandma refers to alcohol as medicine, saying, "He doesn't have the pills to ease him, God help us, and a bottle of stout will be some small comfort." When Malachy's friends wish to show their sympathy, they do so by buying him drinks. Drink is also portrayed as the elixir that gives men the freedom to express emotion. Frank reveals that as a child he thought men could cry "only when you have the black stuff that is called the pint."

In Chapter II, we see Frank becoming a strong-willed man. Although he is young, he is the oldest child in his family. At times, he even serves as his father's babysitter: he goes to the pubs with his father and insists that they leave at a reasonable hour; he goes to the pubs to fetch his father and refuses to leave until his father comes with him.

CHAPTER III

SUMMARY

Angela decides to move her family from Harstonge Street to a house on Roden Lane, because the room on Harstonge Street reminds her too much of Eugene. The St. Vincent de Paul Society gives the family some secondhand furniture. When they move into their new place, the McCourts discover that eleven families use the lavatory that's built next to their house. Malachy wants to hang up his picture of Pope Leo XIII, whom he identifies as a friend of the workingman. While driving a nail into the wall to hang the picture, he cuts his hand and drips blood onto the picture.

Angela despairs at the reduced sixteen shillings a week that the family has to live on. Because Eugene and Oliver have died, the family gets less money from public assistance. Malachy McCourt Sr. takes himself off on long walks into the countryside and looks for work. When he does find work, he drinks away his earnings. In his mind, the dole money goes to his family, and the money he earns with a day's work on a farm goes to the bar.

Two weeks before Christmas, Frank and Malachy return from school to find that the first floor of their house has flooded. The family moves into the upstairs room, which they nickname "Italy" because it is warm and dry. Angela goes to the butcher's to get meat for Christmas, but all she is able to obtain with her grocery dockets is a pig's head. As they carry home the meat, Frank's classmates see them and laugh at their poverty. Frank's father is disgusted that Frank had to carry the head home. He considers carrying things through the streets undignified, and refuses to do it himself.

On Christmas morning, Malachy and Frank attend Mass with their father and go to collect leftover coal strewn over the Dock Road so that their mother can cook the pig's head. Pa Keating meets the boys on the street and convinces the landlord of South's pub to give them a bag of real coal. They drag the coal home through the rain, passing cozy houses. Children laugh at them from inside the houses, taunting them and calling them "Zulus" because they are smeared with black coal. When they get home, Angela cooks the pig's head, and the family has a jolly Christmas dinner.

Angela gives birth to a baby, Michael, whom Frank's father says was left by an angel on their seventh stair. Frank names this seraph the "Angel on the Seventh Step," and annoys his father by asking lots of questions on this and other topics. Angela returns from hospital with Michael, who is sick with a cold. When the baby stops breathing, Frank's father saves his life by sucking the mucus out of his nose.

Men from the welfare society turn up and inspect the house. Angela asks the men for boots for her sons, prompting an irritable comment from her husband that she should "never beg like that." She asks if he'd prefer that the boys go barefoot. To prove to her that he can fix their shoes, Frank's father mends the boys' boots using pieces of old tire. The next day, Frank and Malachy's schoolmates taunt them for wearing ridiculous-looking boots. Frank's schoolmaster tells his class that no one in the class is rich, that you don't see Jesus "on the cross sporting shoes," and that he will whip anyone who continues to tease the McCourts.

Frank talks to the Angel on the Seventh Step and tells him all the things he dislikes about his school. His father overhears and laughs with Angela.

Frank describes the unemployed men in Limerick, who sit and smoke cigarettes when the weather is good because they are "worn out" after collecting their dole and sitting around doing nothing for the rest of the day. He describes the men's wives, who let their husbands sit on the chairs because the men have been out collecting the dole while the women have been home, cooking and cleaning and minding the children.

On Easter morning, Frank attends Mass with his father. He is frustrated by what he does not understand, and by his father's refusal to answer his many questions. His father tells him that he will understand when he grows up. Frank wants to become an adult as soon as possible so that he can "understand everything."

Frank's father gets a job at the Limerick cement factory. The new job pleases Angela, and on payday she wakes up early to clean the house and sing. Frank and Malachy look forward to going to the movies, but they are disappointed when their father does not come home on Friday night with his wages. When Angela realizes that he has gone to the pub, she starts crying and goes to bed. Frank and Malachy listen as their father returns home, drunkenly singing folk songs about dying for Ireland, as he always does after a night at the pub. Frank and Malachy reject the "Friday Penny" that their father offers them and watch as Angela tells him to sleep downstairs. The chapter ends with a long sentence stating that "Dad" missed work in the morning, lost his job, and had to go back on the dole.

ANALYSIS

The McCourts are plagued in turn by rats, flies, human waste, and water. Nevertheless, Frank is unfazed. He describes with equanimity the terrible odor emanating from the street toilet, the flooding of his house, and Michael's near-death experience. Not much perturbs him. We are keenly aware of the suffering taking place, however, especially since at two points in the chapter the boys have occasion to ask their father what "affliction" means. The first time Malachy answers, "Sickness, son, and things that don't fit"; the second, "The world is an affliction and everything in it."

Frank's perspective is endearing, because in contrast to the closed mentalities and downtrodden spirits of those around him, his mind is open to all avenues of thought. We see his imagination when he talks to the Angel on the Seventh Step. We see his kindness when the pig's head evokes not his embarrassment but overwhelmingly his sadness, because the pig is dead and people are laughing at it. We see his curiosity when he asks about Jesus' crown of thorns and questions the justness of an angel who allows a baby to fall ill.

McCourt satirizes his own childhood wish to grow up and "understand everything" like an adult. The underlying point is that grown-ups understand little more than children do. McCourt juxtaposes Frank's youthful enthusiasm with the complacency of those grown-ups—such as the men of the Labour Exchange—who sit around smoking, drinking, and judging the world. The author thus records the faults of adult society through a child's eyes.

Because of his poverty, Frank is constantly teased or treated unkindly. In the beginning of the chapter, when the welfare officer says "beggars can't be choosers," we realize that, for the McCourts, this is not a cliché but reality. Frank's schoolmates tease him as he carries the pig's head, saying that the only part of the pig the McCourts don't eat is "the oink." Frank and Malachy get teased as they walk, dripping with rain and coal, through the streets. Frank gets teased for his shoes mended with tires. Because his father is too dignified to ask for new boots for the boys, Frank finds himself in no-man's-land. He is not like the boys rich enough to buy new boots and not like the shoeless boys. As he says, "If you have rubber tires on your shoes you're all alone with your brother and you have to fight your own battles."

The theme of respect dominates this chapter, as Frank's father struggles to preserve his own dignity. When foremen refuse to hire Malachy because they are biased against Northerners, Frank's father refuses to feign a Limerick accent. He also refuses to go out without a collar and tie, even though Angela suggests that he would be hired more readily if he looked like a workingman. Angela terms Malachy's need to look dignified the "Grand Manner." When Frank's father declares that it is below his dignity to beg or to carry anything through the streets, we see that Malachy's first priority is to protect his own self-esteem. Because Malachy drinks the money away, someone must beg, and someone must carry pig's heads through the streets; the fact that Malachy refuses to do these things simply means that they get done by his pregnant wife and small sons. Although Malachy would prefer that everyone in his family retain his or her dignity, he would rather put his wife and children to work than compromise his own self-regard.

But again, in this chapter, Frank does not wholly condemn his father. Malachy eats almost nothing on Christmas Day so that his sons might fill their bellies, and he clearly adores his family despite his bad behavior.

McCourt draws our attention to the vast unfairness of gender roles. In an unusual passage, he casts off his tone of detached amusement, angrily and sarcastically describing the lazy, ruminative men who do nothing but collect the dole, then sit around filling the day one way or another. He draws a contrast between their ease and the hard lives of their wives, who must cook and clean and take care of the children. Most offensive to him, he implies, is that everyone, including the women, thinks that it is the husbands who work hard and the wives who do little. The society is so entrenched in these ideas that no one notices what is right in front of them: the women are the ones working, the women are the ones bearing the brunt of the poverty and the demands of the children. This anger recurs in the image of Angela and her sons struggling up the hill with their shameful pig's head; the pregnant mother's back aching; the boys tormented by their classmates; and the father safe at home, wrapped up in his dignity and so excused from lifting a finger to help.

When Malachy does get a job, we all—the readers and the McCourts—know he will lose it. The chapter ends with the sentence "He makes his way downstairs with the candle, sleeps on a chair, misses work in the morning, loses the job at the cement factory, and we're back on the dole again." The rapid-fire delivery suggests that because the McCourts have been through this familiar sequence so many times before it needs no explanation, and that jobs can be lost and hopes dashed in the space of a single sentence.

CHAPTER IV

SUMMARY

> The master says it's a glorious thing to die for the
> Faith and Dad says it's a glorious thing to die for
> Ireland and I wonder if there's anyone in the world
> who would like us to live.   (See QUOTATIONS, p. 54)

Crossed-eyed Mikey Molloy, who is eleven years old, lives in Frank's neighborhood. He knows about the female body and "Dirty Things in General." Mikey's mother, Nora, is often admitted to the lunatic asylum because her husband frequently drinks away all of the money, leaving her frantic about how to feed her family. Before she is taken away, Nora obsessively bakes bread to ensure that her children do not starve while she is gone. It is unclear to what degree Nora is actually crazed and to what degree she enjoys getting some peace and quiet at the asylum.

Frank's First Communion, the first time he eats the Communion wafer, is about to take place. Mikey is not a "proper" Catholic because he could never swallow the Communion wafer. Mikey tells Frank that the best things about your First Communion day are that you receive money from your neighbors and you get to go to the movies and eat sweets.

Frank's new schoolmaster is called Mr. Benson. Mr. Benson teaches his pupils the catechism. He is an enthusiastic Catholic, but he dislikes answering questions. One boy, Brendan "Question" Quigley, is constantly in trouble for asking too many of them. Another boy in Frank's class is Paddy Clohessy, who is impoverished and wears no shoes. Frank recalls the day he found a raisin in his pastry at school. Everyone begged him for the treat, but he saw Paddy looking dogged and hungry, and gave it to him.

McCourt places scenes of the schoolboys learning their catechism by rote alongside a scene of his friends and him sitting under the streetlights, reading their own books. Mikey tells his friends about the great Cuchulain's wife, Emer, who was the "champion woman pisser of Ireland" and won her husband in a pissing contest. Frank worries that he has committed a terrible sin by listening to this tale and asks the Angel on the Seventh Step what to do. Frank's seraph tells him not to be afraid, that he should confess his sin to the priest and he will be forgiven. Frank asks his father what he should do, and Malachy reassures him that listening to a rude tale is not a sin, but that he can confess to it if it will make him feel better.

Things go smoothly for Frank at his First Confession: the priest is secretly amused by the Cuchulain story and absolves the boy of his sins, although he warns Frank that books can be "dangerous for children." However, the next day Angela and Grandma bring Frank to the church late. He has trouble swallowing the Communion wafer. When he returns to his grandmother's house, he eats breakfast and then throws it up in her backyard. Grandma frets that she has "God in me backyard" and drags Frank back to church to confess and to find out what she should do. The amused priest tells Frank to wash away the mess with a little water, but he gets annoyed when Frank's grandmother makes Frank ask whether she should use holy or ordinary water. Due to these events, Frank misses his Collection (the money-collecting ritual of First Communion) and does not have any money to go to the movies. However, Mikey pretends to have a fit, and while the ticket man is attending to him, Frank sneaks into the cinema.

ANALYSIS

We get a bit of comic relief in this chapter. Nothing dire happens to the McCourt family, and the descriptions of poverty and despair center on the Molloy family. Frank can see humor in his neighbors' problems that he can't see in his own.

McCourt draws a comparison between received knowledge, such as the information passed from schoolmaster to pupil, and found knowledge, such as the information gleaned from reading and talking to peers. Mikey Molloy's coarse stories and sexual expertise are particularly fascinating to Frank, but both ways of learning are tinged with fear. Frank worries that he has sinned by listening to dirty stories, and Mr. Benson accompanies his teaching with constant threats of murder and mayhem if the boys do not do as he wishes.

Frank's Angel represents the understanding friend that Frank needs. McCourt characterizes the Angel as unambiguously real: he appears to Frank as a light in his head and a voice in his ear.

Frank confesses with great alacrity to the smallest of sins, such as listening to the Cuchulain story. This rigorous confessing is touching, since Frank seems relatively free from sin, but it demonstrates Frank's desire to be good and shows how confusing the world is for children. McCourt balances the naïve worldview of the narrator with an adult's ironic and often self-deprecating wit. For example, we chuckle along with the adult McCourt at the thought of Grandma spitting on Frank's head to flatten his "Presbyterian" hair, and fretting over God in her backyard.

CHAPTER V

SUMMARY

Frank explains the snubs and silent treatments that are a constant presence in his neighborhood. These resentments can be long-held: a family might have alienated itself hundreds of years ago by helping the English or by converting to Protestantism to avoid dying from starvation. It is said that those in the latter group converted for a bowl of soup, and so they are called "soupers."

McCourt contrasts the lack of communication within his own family (his grandmother doesn't speak to his mother, his mother doesn't talk to her siblings, his father doesn't talk to Angela's family, and no one talks to his uncle's wife) with Angela's conversations with her neighbor Bridey Hannon, which are open and affectionate.

During one of the conversations, Angela recites a poem that reminds her of herself and Malachy, because its subject is a girl and her lover from the north of Ireland. Frank notes in bewilderment that his mother "goes into hysterics" over the poem's ironies, particularly the third verse:

> But there's not—and I say it with joy and with pride
> A better man in all Munster wide
> And Limerick town has no happier hearth
> Than mine has been with my man from the North.

Malachy writes letters for neighbors, who exclaim over his nice handwriting and his way with language.

A Protestant man, Bill Galvin, moves into Frank's grandmother's house on the advice of Uncle Pat. Angela persuades her mother to let Frank deliver Bill's lunch every day at the limekiln. Frank is so hungry that he eats Bill's lunch on the first day; in consequence, he has to deliver the lunch for two weeks without pay.

In part because of their constant smoking, Angela and Malachy must get their teeth pulled and buy false teeth. As a joke, Frank's brother Malachy puts his father's set of false teeth in his mouth, and they get stuck. He must be rushed to the hospital to have them removed. The doctor sees Frank breathing with his mouth open and determines that Frank needs to have his tonsils removed.

The chapter takes a humorous turn when Angela tells Frank that he is to take Irish dance lessons every Saturday. Frank feels foolish at his first class, and he spends the money for his next lesson going to the movies with Billy Campbell. He continues skipping classes and using the money to go to the movies and eat sweets. When he gets home after his trips to the theater, he invents his own dances so that his parents won't suspect his ruse. Angela and Malachy finally confront their son after his teacher sends them a note asking where he has been. Malachy forces Frank to confess his sins to a priest.

Three years pass with this sentence: "I'm seven, eight, nine going on ten and still Dad has no work." Malachy constantly loses jobs because on Friday night he drinks away his weekly pay, and then he oversleeps and misses work on Saturday. Angela discusses her woes with Bridey Hannon as the two women sit around the fireplace smoking Woodbine cigarettes.

Frank has to join the Arch Confraternity of the Redemptorist Church in Limerick so that his mother can tell the St. Vincent de

ANGELA'S ASHES ❧ 29
Paul Society of his membership and impress them with the fact that
she is raising her boys to be good Catholics. Members of the Confraternity must go to every meeting or risk getting in trouble with
Father Gorey, which would shame the member's family. Frank's
prefect, Declan Collopy, boasts that his own service for the Confraternity will help him get a job selling linoleum.

Malachy wants Frank to be an altar boy. He spends hours teaching his son the Latin Mass, which he has memorized. Frank and
Malachy go to the church one day and ask the man who comes to
the door whether Frank might become an altar boy. The man looks
at Frank and Malachy, says there's no room, and slams the door.
Angela blames this behavior on class snobbery.

ANALYSIS

Malachy's intelligence becomes apparent in this chapter. He writes
letters for people in the neighborhood, most of whom are illiterate,
and everyone commends him for his lovely handwriting and com-
mand of the English language. He also knows the Latin Mass in it
entirety. He is a natural scholar, demonstrating his reverence for
words when he says, "Latin is sacred and it is to be learned and
recited on the knees."

As Frank matures, he begins to notice the vagaries of religion and
class. He reports on some of the perceived differences between
Catholic and Protestant, and although he simply observes the differences without commenting, the observation itself is significant. He
notes that heathens go to hell, along with all of the Protestants, and
that there is a specific place in hell reserved for the soupers (Catholics turned Protestant to avoid starvation during the Great Famine).
Frank seems a bit baffled that his neighbors hold grudges based on
religious conversions that happened hundreds of years ago. Also,
Frank senses his father's heartbreaking pride in his son, and his subsequent disappointment when, because of class, Frank is not
allowed to become an altar boy.

For the first time, Frank overhears his mother talking at length
about her worries. Just as Frank's consciousness of class and religion is growing, his consciousness of his parents' psychologies is, as
well. When Angela complains that her husband can't behave like the
other husbands and jokes to Bridey Hannon that her life is a hell,
Frank begins to understand his mother more fully. He realizes that
"the fag [cigarette] is the only comfort they have."

Frank endures poverty as a part of life. He accepts uncomplainingly his punishment for eating Bill Galvin's lunch, even though extreme hunger drove him to do it. Nevertheless, he sees that his family lacks even the most basic luxuries: movies and candy for Frank, cigarettes for Angela, drink for Malachy. Only Frank's father indulges himself without restraint; Angela has to beg for her cigarettes from the woman at the grocery store, and Frank has to steal from his parents in order to go to the movies.

CHAPTERS VI–VII

SUMMARY: CHAPTER VI

At school, Frank is now in the fourth form, which is taught by Mr. O'Neill, a tiny man with a passion for geometry. Mr O'Dea, the fifth-form master, is infuriated when he finds from Paddy Clohessy that Mr. O'Neill is teaching the boys about Euclid and geometry, because geometry is not supposed to be taught until the fifth form. The headmaster orders Mr. O'Neill to stop teaching it.

Every day, Mr. O'Neill gives his apple peel, a great delicacy, to the boy who correctly answers a difficult question. One day, this honor falls to Fintan Slattery, whom Frank describes as a dandified do-gooder. Fintan goes to church every day with his mother; he curls his blond hair and answers taunts with a saintly smile. Fintan shares the peel with Frank, Quigley, and Paddy Clohessy. This humiliates the boys, who do not want to be associated with the feminine Fintan. Fintan invites Paddy and Frank to his house after school, luring them with promises of food. Fintan's mother serves milk and sandwiches with mustard, luxurious treats for the boys. Paddy and Frank are worried, however, by the fact that Fintan goes with them to the bathroom and says he enjoys looking at them.

A few days later, Fintan invites the boys home with him for lunch, but instead of feeding them, he eats his sandwich by himself. Angry and hungry, Paddy and Frank don't return to school after lunch, but cut class to steal apples and milk from a nearby farm. Quigley sees Frank and tells him his parents are looking for him and are going to kill him. Scared, Frank goes home with Paddy, who lives in unbearable squalor. Paddy's father is consumptive and lies in bed coughing up green fluid into a bucket. The next morning, Angela appears with the school guard and tells Frank how worried she has been about him. Mr. Clohessy reminisces with Angela, remembering how they used to dance together. Angela sings for the dying man and cries as she leaves his home, sorry for Mr. Clohessy's sickness and sad to remember the carefree times they had when they were young. Frank is sorry for Mr. Clohessy, but he is mostly relieved not to be in trouble.

SUMMARY: CHAPTER VII

Malachy continues to drink away his dole money. The brothers, even three-year-old Michael, take their cue from Angela and refuse to talk to Malachy during the weekend after he drinks the dole.

Frank has a friend named Mickey Spellacy whose siblings are dying of consumption one by one. Everyone envies Mickey because he gets a week off from school for every sibling that dies, and money and sympathy from grown-ups who feel sorry for him. Mickey asks Frank and Billy Campbell to pray that Mickey's sick sister will not die until September, so that Mickey can get a week off from school. In return, Mickey promises Frank and Billy that they will be invited to his sister's wake, where there will be food and singing and stories. Although Mickey gets his wish, and his sister dies during the school term, the boys are not invited to the wake. Frank is satisfied when Mickey himself dies of consumption the following year and doesn't get any time off from school.

Grandma decides Frank should help Uncle Pat deliver newspapers. Uncle Pat mistreats Frank, making him run about in the rain, and paying him poorly. Frank delivers the paper to an old man named Mr. Timoney, and agrees to read to him for money. Mr. Timoney is a smart, well-traveled, crotchety old man, and he takes to Frank. At Timoney's request, Frank reads John Swift's satirical essay "A Modest Proposal." Angela tells Frank that Mr. Timoney served in the English army in India and married an Indian woman who was accidentally killed by a soldier. Angela is thrilled that her son now has two jobs, but Frank gets in trouble with Declan Collopy for missing the Confraternity's Friday night meetings. Declan insults Uncle Pat, and Frank fights Declan. Mr. Timoney vows to talk to Pa Keating about Declan's bullying. It is a relief to Frank to have the companionship of Mr. Timoney, who talks to him like a friend would. A little later, however, Mr. Timoney is pronounced demented and taken away to the City Home because he laughed when his dog bit three people and when a priest pronounced his Buddhism a danger to Catholics.

In the summer, Angela gives birth to a boy. Bridey Hannon's mother saves the child from choking to death on a ball of dried milk.

Angela decides to name the baby Alphonsus, a name Frank dislikes. Grandpa sends his new grandson a money order for five pounds. Angela sends Malachy to get the money order cashed, and she sends Frank and Malachy Jr. with their father to watch him. After Malachy gets the cash, he orders the boys home. They protest, but he walks away from them and into the pub. Angela, incensed, sends them back out to find him. While searching the Limerick pubs, Frank steals a drunken man's fish and chips. Feeling guilty for the theft, he goes to Confession right away. The priest asks him why he stole, and when it comes out that Frank was hungry because his father is out drinking up all the money for food, the priest says he (the priest) should be washing the feet of those he hears confess, not doling out penances.

Frank goes back out into the night and eventually hears his father singing in a pub. Frank is "raging inside," but he thinks of mornings by the fire with his father and of the look in his father's eyes when he drinks: "he has that look in his eyes Eugene had when he searched for Oliver." Frank goes home with Malachy, thinking that everything will change now, because it is one thing to drink your wages and the dole money, but drinking money meant for a baby is "beyond the beyonds."

ANALYSIS: CHAPTERS VI–VII

In Chapter VI, we see how children soak up the political views and opinions of their parents, and take them for their own. When Paddy Clohessy scoffs, "The English quality wouldn't give you the steam of their piss," and Frank is impressed by his cleverness, Paddy admits that the saying comes directly from his father, who complains about the English as he lies dying in his bed. Hatred of the English, among other things, is taught to these children every day.

When Frank goes to Paddy's house, we feel, along with Frank, relief that the McCourts live in relative comfort. As Frank says to himself, "It's bad when our kitchen is a lake and we have to go up to Italy but it's worse in the Clohessys' when you have to go down four flights to the lavatory and slip on shit all the way down."

As usual, death hovers over daily life. It is such an omnipresent part of Frank's existence that he feels little more than grim satisfaction when the annoying Mickey Spellacy dies of consumption.

In Chapter VII, McCourt draws a contrast between the masters' narrow-minded teaching (their squabbling over who owns Euclid and geometry) and Mr. Timoney's freethinking curiosity. Mr. Timoney, an anti-establishment figure, is instantly appealing and lovable. He is full of life, yelling at his dog and calling her an "old hoor," touting the virtues of Buddhism, and recognizing Frank's intelligence and treating him like a peer. Because Timoney exists at the edges of normal society, however, people look on him with suspicion and distrust. McCourt suggests that Mr. Timoney is taken to the Home because of his eccentricity, wisdom, and religious difference, rather than for any real mental illness.

Mr. Timoney introduces Frank to Jonathan Swift's work "A Modest Proposal," in which Swift uses satire to highlight the plight of the Irish poor. Although Frank does not understand what he is reading, the allusion to this text reminds readers that Swift was satirizing hunger such as that from which Frank suffers.

In past chapters, Frank has noted what the reader recognizes as the foibles of the Catholic church, citing its condemnatory policies, even though he takes them for universal truth and does not question them. In this chapter, though, Frank experiences the love and charity of Catholicism when he visits a priest and confesses to stealing food. The priest says, "My child, I sit here. I hear the sins of the poor. I assign the penance. I bestow absolution. I should be on my knees washing their feet." The priest is kind, wise, and truly compassionate, and his words reference the actions of Jesus, who knelt to wash the feet of his apostles.

A turning point comes when Malachy drinks away the baby's money. This marks the first time Frank expresses real anger about his father's staggering irresponsibility. Although he thinks of sitting by his father before the fire and hearing stories, and although he realizes that when Malachy drinks he is somehow looking for his dead children, Frank also "rages inside," and he wants to run into the bar and kick his father. Frank himself recognizes this anger as a turning point, saying, "[I]t will be different now."

CHAPTER VIII

SUMMARY

I know when Dad does the bad thing. I know when he drinks the dole money and Mam is desperate and has to beg . . . but I don't want to back away from him and run to Mam.   (See QUOTATIONS, p. 55)

Frank is ten years old and preparing for his Confirmation. Peter Dooley, whom everyone calls "Quasimodo" because of his hunched back, offers to let Frank, Billy Campbell, and Mikey Molloy pay a shilling to look at his naked sisters. The day before their Confirmation, they go to Peter's house. Mikey Molloy climbs the drainpipe to see the girls, but, as he masturbates, he starts to have a fit and falls off the pipe. Quasimodo's mother appears, shuts Quasimodo in the coal cellar, and berates the boys for looking at her daughters. She tells Angela that Frank should go to Confession before his Confirmation the next day, but Angela says she won't have him prevented from being Confirmed just because "he climbed a spout for an innocent gawk at the scrawny arse of Mona Dooley." She drags Frank home and makes him swear in front of the picture of the pope that he didn't see Mona naked.

The next day, Frank is Confirmed. Afterward, he gets a nosebleed that will not stop. He feels too sick to make his Collection. Some days later, the doctor visits Frank at home and diagnoses him with typhoid fever. Frank goes to the hospital, and for days he drifts in and out of consciousness. He is close to death and is given the rites of Extreme Unction. However, a few days later a doctor farts in front of him, and Frank realizes that he will live, thinking that a doctor would never fart in front of a dying boy.

Frank's father visits him and kisses him on the forehead for the first time in his life, which makes the boy so happy that he feels like "floating" out of bed.

During his stay in the hospital, Frank meets a girl named Patricia Madigan, who is dying of diphtheria. The two children befriend Seamus, an old man who cleans the hospital. Patricia lends Frank a history book, in which he reads his first two lines of Shakespeare. The beauty of Shakespeare's language overwhelms Frank. He says speaking the lines is like "having jewels in [his] mouth." Patricia recites part of Alfred Noyes's poem "The Highwayman." The nurse is infuriated to find the two children talking, and she tells the nun in charge, who moves Frank into another ward, saying, "Diphtheria is never allowed to talk to typhoid." Frank overhears the nurse talking to Seamus about all of the children who died of starvation in that very ward during the potato famine. She also tells Seamus that Patricia does not have long to live. Two days later, Seamus tells Frank that Patricia died as she was trying to make her way to the bathroom.

Frank asks Seamus to find out what happens at the end of "The Highwayman." Seamus asks around at the pub, finds someone who knows the poem, and memorizes it so he can report to Frank. It turns out that at the end of the poem, both the hero and his lover die. During the rest of his stay in hospital, Frank reads books.

Frank is allowed to return home fourteen weeks after his eleventh birthday and is greeted warmly by the people in his street. On his return to school in November, Frank is disappointed to learn that he has to repeat the fifth year instead of moving up to the sixth with his friends. Although he is barely strong enough to walk there, Frank clings to walls and eventually reaches the statue of St. Francis of Assisi, where he gives a penny to light a candle, and prays to be moved to the sixth form. Shortly thereafter, he writes an impressive essay on what would have happened had Jesus grown up in Limerick, which persuades Mr. O'Dea to move him up to the sixth class. Frank is amazed by his new teacher, Mr. O'Halloran, who encourages questions and admits that the Irish, as well as the English, committed atrocities during the Battle of Kinsale. Frank concludes his teacher must be telling the truth because he is also the headmaster.

Frank feels mixed emotions about his father. He dislikes it when Malachy drinks his dole money, but he loves his mornings alone with his father, when they read the paper and talk; he loves the stories his father tells. In this chapter, Malachy talks for the first time about school, telling Frank how in the old days the English closed Irish schools in order to keep the people ignorant, and how the Irish attended school secretly, in ditches. He also tells Frank that if he could, he would go to America and get an office job, saying, "America is not like Limerick, a gray place with a river that kills."

Except for the protagonist's return to the hospital to eat Christmas dinner, the rest of this chapter focuses on the terrible odors emanating from the lavatory right outside the McCourts' door. Along with these smells, the family is plagued by rats and flies. Frank is saddened by the death of Finn the Horse, who lived in the stable close to his house.

SUMMARY & ANALYSIS

ANALYSIS

Running through this chapter is a current of anti-English sentiment. McCourt implies that as Frank grows older, he becomes increasingly aware of how much the grown-ups around him detest the English. Seamus thinks it's a shame that Frank is reading a history of England, and that there are no histories of Ireland in the hospital. The nurse speaks of the "children suffering and dying here while the English feasted on roast beef and guzzled the best of wine in their big houses, little children with their mouths all green from trying to eat the grass in the fields beyond." Despite the constant display of anti-English sentiment, this chapter also marks the first expression of an evenhanded examination of English-Irish relations. Mr. O'Halloran's admission that the Irish committed atrocities is the first such admission Frank has heard, and it shocks him.

Another theme of this chapter is storytelling. It is now that Frank discovers the deliciousness of stories, and fiction bursts into bloom like a garden with all varieties of flowers: a line of Shakespeare, a history of England, a poem read from a book, a pub song, articles in the newspaper, Irish history, social satires by P. G. Wodehouse, fantastical stories from Malachy, and a sharp and touching essay by Frank. This outpouring of fiction is the autobiography's first display of riches or abundance of any kind, and it comes as a relief to Frank and to the reader.

When Patricia dies, Frank is less disturbed by the fact of her death than by the fact that she will not be able to tell him how "The Highwayman" ends. His reaction to her death may seem callous, but it reminds the reader that Frank has had much more exposure to death than he has to poetry, and so for him, poetry is more powerful and moving even than death.

Frank's understanding of his father continues to grow. When talking of his mixed feelings for Malachy, he says, "I think my father is like the Holy Trinity with three people in him, the one in the morning with the paper, the one at night with the stories and the prayers, and then the one who does the bad thing and comes home with the smell of whiskey and wants us to die for Ireland." Frank demonstrates both that he understands his father and that he understands a subtle point of Catholic theology, which holds that God is three people in one—Father, Son, and Holy Spirit.

CHAPTERS IX–X

SUMMARY: CHAPTER IX

> *Mam turns toward the dead ashes in the fire....*
> *Michael who is only five ... wants to know if we're*
> *having fish and chips tonight because he's hungry.*
> *Mam says, Next week, love, and he goes back out to*
> *play in the lane.* (See QUOTATIONS, p. 56)

Angela announces that she's done having children. Because birth control was not commonly used at that time in households such as the McCourts', this is tantamount to refusing sex. Malachy is annoyed that she will not perform her "wifely duties."

Families up and down the lane are getting richer because the fathers are off in England, fighting in World War II. After Angela threatens to go to England herself to find work, Frank's father decides to leave for England and find work in a munitions factory. The family sees Malachy off at the station, and Angela promises the boys one egg apiece on Sunday mornings once their father's money starts coming. An egg a week seems an unimaginable luxury to Frank. Angela tells Bridey Hannon that with the money Malachy will send she wants to get a new house, electric lighting, coats and boots for the boys, and food. However, Malachy fails to send any money. Every Friday, families up and down the lane get money orders from England, but the McCourt family never gets anything.

Angela learns from Bridey that the Meagher family receives public assistance from the Dispensary, which Frank's mother considers a terrible shame. She says getting public assistance is far worse than the dole or the St. Vincent de Paul Society, because it means you are one step away from putting your children in an orphanage and begging on the street.

Frank gets an infection in his eyes, which Grandma blames on his constant reading, and Angela has to take him to the Dispensary to see the doctor. The doctor says Frank has the worst case of conjunctivitis he has ever seen, and sends Frank to the hospital.

In the hospital, Frank sees both Seamus and Mr. Timoney, who seems to have aged greatly—Timoney is muted, not his old vivacious self, although he tells Frank to rest his eyes and then "read till they fall out of your head." Seamus visits Frank three times a week and recites poetry to him, but soon leaves to work in an English factory.

When Frank returns home, he discovers that his father has "gone pure mad with the drink," spending all of his money in bars. Angela becomes desperate and decides to go to the Dispensary for public assistance. Once there, she is humiliated by a sanctimonious official called Mr. Kane, who accuses her of claiming aid her family does not deserve.

SUMMARY: CHAPTER X

The family moves upstairs to escape the cold and wet. Angela soon sickens and turns feverish, calling out for lemonade. Frank steals two bottles of lemonade from a crate outside South's pub and a loaf of bread from a van parked outside O'Connell's grocery store. To entertain his brothers, Frank embellishes the story of how he got the food and drink, and Michael calls him an outlaw. Malachy says Frank is no different from Robin Hood, who steals from the rich and gives to the poor. The next day, Frank steals a whole box of food that has been delivered to a house in a wealthy area of town. The boys have enough food, but no fire. They go to a rich neighborhood and go door to door asking for turf or coal, but no one will help them, and they soon resort to stealing fuel from people's back gardens.

A guard soon appears at their home to find out why the boys have been absent from school. The official tells Frank to get his Grandma and Aunt Aggie, who in turn send for the doctor. The doctor diagnoses Angela with pneumonia and drives her to hospital, while the McCourt brothers go to stay with Aggie.

Although Pa Keating is kind to his nephews and gives them food, Aggie constantly abuses the boys, hitting them and yelling at them. The protagonist writes to his father and explains that his mother is in the hospital. Malachy returns to Limerick to look after his sons, but he leaves for England again the day after Angela gets back from the hospital. Because Frank's father only sends one of his paychecks home, Angela is soon forced to appeal to the Dispensary for money again. Frank's sadness at their situation turns into despair when he sees his mother begging for food outside a church. Frank is so ashamed that he is hardly able to look at his mother, whom he describes as a "beggar."

ANALYSIS: CHAPTERS IX–X

Grandma berates the protagonist for ruining his eyes with "[b]ooks, books, books," but reading offers Frank a temporary escape from the world's miseries.

We see again in Chapter IX that dignity is of paramount importance to Angela. Although the McCourts have no money and live in squalor, Angela is determined to save them from a low-class mentality. She criticizes mothers who call their children in to dinner and name the menu, announcing their riches to the lane. She says it is not classy to show off that way.

Out of respect and pride, the McCourts do not criticize their father in public, however much he deserves it. One boy calls his father, who never sends money from England, "a drunken oul' shit," but Angela and her boys would never speak of Malachy in such a way. This good behavior may not help the family get enough food to eat or enough coal to heat their house, but it keeps their standards high.

The men in charge of giving out money and charity constantly humiliate their impoverished customers. It's not enough that the impoverished are poor, it's not enough that they are humiliated already because they must beg for assistance, it's not enough that the men torment them—they are also required to laugh along with their tormenters, or risk foregoing aid. When Frank waits to get his eyes checked, he sees the men in charge making fun of a woman in pain, suggesting that she has gas or has eaten too much cabbage. The woman must laugh with the men and pretend that she finds their rudeness amusing, or else she will not get to see a doctor. When the McCourts go to get public assistance, the men are sadistic, saying, "The public assistance, is that what you want, woman, the relief?" When it comes Angela's turn to ask for aid, the men humiliate her by saying she does not deserve it, because her husband is from the North and she is ignorant.

When Frank's mother falls ill in Chapter X, Frank is quick to assume responsibility for his family's welfare. As the guard who visits the house points out, Frank will make a good father someday.

CHAPTERS XI–XII

SUMMARY: CHAPTER XI

Frank decides to start a soccer team with his brother Malachy and his friend Billy Campbell. Frank remembers a red flapper dress his mother bought in New York, which she keeps to remind her of her dancing days, and the dress inspires him with a name for the team: "The Red Hearts of Limerick." Frank takes the dress from its place in an old trunk and cuts red hearts out of it for the uniforms. While looking in the trunk, Frank finds some old papers. He looks through them and learns from the date on his parents' marriage certificate that he was born only six months after they wed. Frank wonders if his was a miraculous birth.

Mikey Molloy has just turned sixteen, and his father, Peter, takes him to the pub for his first pint. The Molloys bring Frank along and buy him a lemonade. Frank asks Mikey what it means that he was born early, and Mikey tells him he is a bastard and is doomed to spend eternity in Limbo. He also explains to Frank how babies are conceived. Frank is worried, and Mikey gives him a penny so he can pay to light a candle and pray to the Virgin Mary to save his soul.

The barman happens to say, "Everything has an opposite," and this sets something off in Peter Molloy, who decides that if he is the pint-drinking champion of Limerick, he could also be "the champion of no pints at all." He tells his son that he'll stop drinking, stop driving his wife mad, and move the family to England. After the Molloys leave, Frank cannot resist using the penny to buy toffee instead of using it to pray for his soul.

On Saturday morning, Frank's team beats a group of rich boys in a soccer game. Frank makes the goal that wins the game, which he decides was divinely ordained to prove Frank is not doomed.

Frank starts delivering coal with his next-door neighbor, Mr. Hannon, who suffers from sores on his legs. Frank feels like a real man, and he loves being able to ride on the float next to Mr. Hannon, who is gentle and kind, and to who urges Frank to go to school and read books and one day leave Ireland for America. One day Hannon waits for him outside his school, and Frank's classmates are jealous of Frank's manly job. They ask Frank if he can put in a good word for them at the coal yard.

Frank's eyes are irritated by the coal dust, and one day they are so bad that even though Mr. Hannon's legs are getting worse and worse, Angela will not let Frank continue working. On the first day that Mr. Hannon would have had to manage alone, his legs are too bad for him to go to work. He is hospitalized, and told he cannot work again. Mrs. Hannon invites Frank over, and tells him that he gave Mr. Hannon "the feeling of a son." Frank cries.

SUMMARY: CHAPTER XII

Frank's father returns home for Christmas, promising that he has turned a new leaf. He arrives a day later than expected and gives his family a box of half-eaten chocolates as a gift. The McCourts eat a sheep's head for their Christmas dinner, and Frank's father leaves after the meal is over.

Frank now takes care to avoid the "respectable boys" while he walks to school. He believes that they will succeed in life, while he and his brothers will end up in jobs that cater to the needs of the upper class. Angela is sickly, and spends most of her time at home. When destitute women approach her and ask if she can spare money, she cannot help but take them home with her and feed them. And Michael, when he sees sick dogs or poor old men, cannot help but invite them home and take care of them. One of the old men brings lice into the house, and for fear of more bugs, or diseases, the family has to agree not to bring home any more strange men or beasts.

Frank's only respite from the grinding poverty is sitting outside Mrs. Purcell's window and listening to Shakespearean plays on her radio. One cold day, she invites him in to listen, and gives him bread with jelly. They listen to Shakespeare and then to other programs, including an American jazz show. Frank dreams of America.

Angela owes four weeks' rent. There is no money, and the family has to burn one of the internal walls for firewood. Angela tells the boys not to touch the beam that supports the roof, but one day when she is out and they are freezing, they cut into it. The roof starts to collapse. Grandma fetches the landlord to fix the roof, but when he sees that the wall is missing, he evicts the McCourts. They go to live with Angela's cousin, Laman Griffin, who used to be an officer in the Royal Navy. Laman is a steady man, holding down a job and going to the pub only on Fridays. However, he humiliates Angela by making her climb up to the loft where he sleeps and clean his chamber pot.

Frank fetches Laman books from the library, and while there Frank is allowed to get a book for himself.

Frank announces abruptly that Grandma has died of pneumonia. Uncle Tom and his wife die of consumption soon afterward. Frank's brother Malachy decides to leave Limerick and join the Army School of Music in Dublin.

ANALYSIS: CHAPTERS XI–XII

Like Mr. Timoney, Mr. Hannon briefly acts as a father figure for Frank. Frank feels love toward Mr. Hannon; he cries to think of "that horse he calls sweet because he's so gentle himself" and to hear Mr. Hannon thinks of him as a son. He does not understand why he cries but knows it has to do with the job or Mr. Hannon.

Mr. Hannon also tells Frank to work hard and get out of Limerick. He tells him that "the world is wide" and he can do anything he likes. This encouragement to be adventurous and ambitious is something Frank rarely hears. McCourt emphasizes its importance to Frank when Mr. Hannon says, "School, Frankie, school. The books, the books, the books." The advice begins to sound mystical, almost like an incantation, and the rhythmic power of Hannon's words suggests the strong affect they have on Frank.

Balancing this advice, however, is Frank's growing shame in his poverty. He begins to think of money as destiny, saying "we know" boys at one school will grow up to be civil servants, "we know" boys at the rich school will grow up to run the world, and "we know" boys at his school will grow up to serve the men in power. The repeated phrase "we know" suggests that Frank is beginning to believe, probably correctly, that for the most part class divisions are carved in stone, that if you are born poor you stay poor, and that hard work will not change your fate.

Frank's anger at his father becomes more overt in these chapters. When he goes with his mother to meet Malachy at the train station and Malachy does not arrive, Frank says, "He's not coming, Mam. He doesn't care about us. He's just drunk over there in England." This statement is the bluntest, and most bitter, remark Frank has ever made about his father. When Malachy does finally show up, all of the boys shout at him, screaming, "You drank the money, Dad," and Malachy, shamefaced, tells them halfheartedly to show respect. By this time, Malachy's behavior, while still painful, is a surprise to no one. When, as usual, he eats almost nothing so that his boys might have more food, the gesture seems less sweet than it used to, and more empty. Loving gestures mean little in the face of wrenching poverty.

CHAPTERS XIII–XIV

SUMMARY: CHAPTER XIII

Frank wants to go on a cycling trip with his friends from school, and convinces Laman to let him borrow his bicycle. In return, he promises to empty Laman's chamber pot every day and to run all of Laman's errands.

One day at the library, the librarian gives Frank a book called *Butler's Lives of the Saints.* The deaths of the virgin martyrs, "worse than any horror film," fascinate Frank. He does not know what the word "virgin" means, and although he looks in the dictionary, the definition is too abstract to be of help. The librarian, Miss O' Riordan, is so impressed by Frank's supposed religious zeal that she writes to congratulate Angela on her son.

Frank's teacher, Mr. O'Halloran, tells Angela that her son is intelligent and must continue school instead of becoming a messenger boy and wasting his talents. On his advice, Angela takes Frank to the Christian Brothers to inquire about further schooling, but the priest there slams the door in the McCourts' faces, telling them that there is no room for Frank. This infuriates Angela.

The post office supervisor offers Frank a job as a telegram messenger. This job offer pleases Frank, who is anxious to finish school. Mr. O'Halloran tells his students that he is disgusted with the class system that forces smart boys into menial jobs, and he tells Frank that he should leave for America. Frank tries to apply to be a chaplain in the Foreign Legion, but his doctor thinks Frank too young and refuses to give him the necessary physical examination.

Frank worries that he is committing a sin by masturbating. He also worries about the fact that his mother is sleeping with Laman Griffin. The day before Frank is due to go on his cycling trip, he forgets to empty Laman's chamber pot. Angered, Laman says that Frank cannot borrow his bike. Frank protests that Laman is breaking his promise, and Laman starts beating Frank. Frank leaves the house and goes to stay with his Uncle Ab Sheehan.

SUMMARY: CHAPTER XIV

Angela sends Michael to Ab Sheehan's house with food for Frank. Michael feels bereft without his big brother, and asks Frank to come home. Frank refuses, but feels guilty. It tears at his heart to watch Michael walk away in his broken shoes and his raggedy clothes, and he thinks of all the things he will buy for Michael once he gets his job at the post office.

Frank spends his days going on long walks in the countryside. He is ashamed that he masturbates, especially when he once masturbates on a hill, "in full view of Ireland."

Uncle Ab refuses to give Frank food, so Frank steals milk and bread from wealthy houses. He concludes that since he is doomed for his sins anyway, a few more will not make any difference. Still, he feels that he is little more than a beggar, standing outside stores and asking for leftover fish and chips.

At the library, Frank happens upon a sex manual written by Lin Yutang, and, after reading it, finally understands the mechanics of intercourse. He says, "My father lied to me for years about the Angel on the Seventh Step." When the shocked librarian discovers that Frank has been reading the manual, she orders him to leave. Frank falls asleep in a park and dreams of virgin martyrs dressed in swimsuits. He wakes up to discover that he is having a wet dream, and people in the park are watching him ejaculate.

Frank returns to Ab's house and washes his clothes in preparation for his first day of work as a messenger boy. He finds a loaf of bread that Ab has hidden in his coat pocket and helps himself to one slice, drinking a glass of water as he eats to make himself feel more full. Because his clothes are still drying and he is cold, Frank puts on an old woolen dress of his grandmother's and goes to bed. His Aunt Aggie brings his drunk uncle home from the pub and finds him in his grandmother's dress. Frank explains and says that he is living with Ab until he can afford to buy a house for his mother and brothers. His aunt concedes that this is "more than your father would do."

ANALYSIS: CHAPTERS XIII–XIV

Although Frank does not comment on Mr. O'Halloran's actions, McCourt makes it clear to the reader that O'Halloran is an inspirational and good man with a keen sense of social injustice. The teacher's indignation at the unfairness of the class system is the first such anger Frank or the reader has heard about Frank's supposed lot in life. For the first time, someone is prompting Frank to think about the unseen forces that keep poor people poor. Although Frank does not explicitly comment on O'Halloran's ideas, he demonstrates that he has noted his teacher's righteous anger; when he reports on O'Halloran's speech, he replicates its fury, saying, "[Mr.

O'Halloran] is disgusted by this free and independent Ireland that keeps a class system foisted on us by the English, [and says] that we are throwing our talented children on the dungheap."

Like Mr. O'Halloran, Angela is angry that Frank cannot get the education he deserves. Angela's anger is directed not at the class system, however, but at the church. In previous chapters there were subtle indications that although Angela brings her boys up as Catholics, she does not embrace the church: she was not the one to take Frank to church on Christmas, and she did not seem overly concerned with the technical cleanliness of Frank's soul prior to his Confirmation. In Chapter XIII, however, she finally voices some of her frustration with the church. She tells Frank, "That's the second time a door was slammed in your face by the Church," and she exhorts him never to let anyone slam a door in his face again.

Frank continues to worry about masturbating, which one priest terms the "vile sin of self-abuse." Although the priests assure the boys that when they masturbate the Virgin Mary weeps, Christ's wounds are reopened, and they take a step toward hell, Frank cannot stop himself from masturbating. His natural urges come into conflict with the stern warnings of the priests, and his guilt deepens.

Frank disapproves of the sexual relationship his mother has with Laman. When Laman beats Frank, Frank thinks that his mother should demonstrate her loyalty to her son by sleeping alone, and he is disgusted when instead, "she cries and begs till there's whispering and grunting and moaning and nothing."

Although young Frank does not fully recognize his mother's pain, McCourt shows the reader how difficult the situation is for Angela. She has no money to buy or rent a place of her own, and so to ensure the survival of her children and keep a roof over their heads, she must stay with Laman and keep him happy. Laman's mistreatment of her children torments Angela. When he laughs and assigns Frank the humiliating job of emptying his chamber pot, Angela "stares into the dead ashes in the fireplace." When Laman beats Frank, Angela screams and protests. Still, she sleeps with Laman on the same night that Laman abuses Frank. McCourt does not make it clear whether their sexual relations are partially a relief to Angela in her loneliness, or whether they are simply an odious duty she feels compelled to perform in order to keep Laman satisfied.

Frank is determined to move to America and to someday provide for his mother and brothers. He would rather "jump into the River Shannon" than give up on his dream.

CHAPTERS XV–XVI

On his fourteenth birthday, Frank goes to the post office to start work, but learns that he is not scheduled to begin until the following Monday. The people working at the office laugh at Frank's raggedy clothes. Aunt Aggie takes her nephew shopping for new clothing, and gives him money to buy a cup of tea and a bun.

The next Monday, Frank starts work. He is a temporary worker, which means that he receives less pay than the permanent workers and cannot stay at his job beyond the age of sixteen. One of the first telegrams he delivers is to Paddy Clohessy's mother. Her house, which used to be a pit of illness and filth, is now filled with new furniture, bright clothes, and good food. She tells Frank that one day after her husband, Dennis, was craving sheep's tongue and Paddy stole one for him, Dennis leaped up and said he refused to die in bed. He went to England, as did Paddy, and both father and son now send money to Mrs. Clohessy. She remarks that were it not for Hitler, she would be dead.

Frank gets his wages, the first pound he has ever had. When Michael tells Frank he is hungry and asks for a scrap of bread, Frank takes Michael to get fish and chips and lemonade, then to a movie, where they eat chocolate, and then out for tea and buns. Afterward, Frank thinks that instead of buying food with his wages, he should save each week so that he can go to America when he turns twenty.

The only people who tip the telegram boys are widows, the poor, and the wives of Protestant ministers. Rich people don't tip, and neither do nuns or priests. Some of the people to whom Frank delivers telegrams are so old and sick that they cannot get out of bed. Although it could cost him his job, Frank helps these people by cashing their money orders and bringing them their groceries.

When school begins, Michael starts staying with Frank in Ab Sheehan's house. Angela comes to see her sons, and goes back to Laman's less and less frequently, until finally she has moved into Ab's altogether. Frank's brother Malachy returns from Dublin a few months later, and the family is reunited. Despite the fact that Frank gives most of his paycheck to Angela, he still enjoys work, since he gets to cycle in the countryside and dream about the future.

One day, Frank delivers a telegram to the house of a seventeen-year-old consumptive girl named Theresa Carmody. Frank arrives soaked with rain, and bloodied from a fall on his bike. Theresa tends to his injuries by putting iodine on his cuts, and tells him to take his pants off to dry by the fire. He does, and when she comes into the room, she leads him to the green couch, where they make love. Theresa is bleeding, and thinking she is cut, Frank pour iodine on her. Frank goes back to see Theresa for weeks, and when Theresa is not too ill, they make love on the couch. One day Frank is told to deliver the telegram to Theresa's mother's workplace. When he does, he learns that Theresa is in the hospital. The next week, Theresa dies. Frank worries that she is in hell because they have had sexual relations outside of marriage, and he fasts and prays and goes to Mass to beg for God to have mercy on Theresa's soul.

SUMMARY: CHAPTER XVI

Frank delivers a condolence telegram to an Englishman named Mr. Harrington, who has lost his wife. Mr. Harrington, who has been drinking, insults the Irish and tries to force Frank to sit and mourn with him. He makes Frank drink sherry. When Mr. Harrington goes to get more alcohol, Frank is left with the corpse. He starts wondering if he can save her, a Protestant, from eternal damnation. He decides to baptize her with the sherry, and as he does this, Mr. Harrington comes back and finds him. Mr. Harrington stuffs a ham sandwich in Frank's mouth, and Frank vomits out the window onto Mrs. Harrington's rosebushes. Frank then escapes by jumping through the window into the rosebushes and vomit below. Mr. Harrington reports Frank and gets him fired, but the priest writes a letter to the post office, and Frank is rehired.

Frank delivers a telegram to an old woman creditor named Mrs. Brigid Finucane. Frank agrees to write bullying letters to her debtors in return for a few shillings. He uses difficult and obscure words in the letters, which intimidate the debtors into paying. Some of the recipients of the letters are Frank's friends and neighbors, and Angela says that whoever is writing the letters should be boiled in oil, but Frank justifies his behavior to himself by thinking of how badly he wants to get to America.

Frank plans to take the exam to get a permanent job at the post office, but Pa Keating sketches out the nice, safe, boring life that would ensue: a wife, five children, and numbness. Pa Keating says, "You'll be dead in your head before you're thirty and dried in your ballocks the year before." Consequently, Frank decides to take a job delivering Protestant newspapers for a man named Mr. McCaffrey.

When Frank's boss, Mrs. O'Connell, hears that Frank walked away from the post office exam, she acts hurt and offended that he fancies himself too good for the postman position.

ANALYSIS: CHAPTERS XV–XVI

Frank makes a crucial realization that he must save part of the money he earns or else face remaining in Limerick forever. It is a mark of Frank's maturity and drive that even though he is nearly starving, he is able to think not of food, and his new ability to buy food, but of the abstract desire to make a new life for himself in America.

Frank continues to grow more conscious of class differences. He sounds bitter when he says, "If you waited for tips from priests or nuns you'd die on their doorstep," and he commiserates with the woman who points out the hypocrisy of those priests and nuns, who drink wine and eat ham and eggs, yet insist that their parishioners should not rail against poverty, since Jesus himself was poor. His job, which takes him to the houses of the sick and impoverished, makes him even more tenderhearted toward the poor. He says it is impossible to refuse anything to a woman who is little more than a pile of old rags, to a man who lost his legs in the war, or to a mother with two crippled children.

The sexual relationship between Frank and Theresa is both lovely and difficult for Frank. The first time they have sex, he describes it this way: "my head is filled with sin and iodine and fear of consumption and the shilling tip and her green eyes and she's on the sofa don't stop or I'll die and she's crying and I'm crying." This description contains all of the complexity of Frank's first sexual experience: it is a sin in the eyes of the Catholic church, Theresa has just tenderly cared for his wounds, she is sick and dying, she is far richer than he, she is beautiful, what they are doing feels good, but the situation is so complicated and emotional that they both cry.

Mr. Harrington tells Frank, with bitter anger, that all Irish people are ghouls, all Irish people are alcoholics, all Irish people whine, all Irish people are starving. When Frank asks for lemonade instead of sherry or whiskey, Harrington forces him to live up to his own stereotypes by foisting sherry on Frank. When Frank refuses a ham sandwich, Harrington literally shoves the food into Frank's mouth to prove himself correct in his idea that all Irish are starving. In a symbolic move, Frank throws up the food Harrington forced on him. It seems that McCourt is suggesting that stereotypes, even those that are rammed down your throat, must be violently cast off. McCourt does not lay the blame entirely at the doorstep of rich Protestants like Mr. Harrington, for when Frank returns to the post office, his version of the story falls on deaf ears. His boss describes Mr. Harrington as a "lovely Englishman that sounds like James Mason." McCourt suggests that Irish people like Frank's boss make the problem worse by accepting Hollywood's version of the English rather than thinking for themselves.

When Pa Keating tells Frank, "Make up your own bloody mind and to hell with the safeshots and the begrudgers," he puts himself in a class with Mr. Timoney and Mr. O'Halloran, men in Frank's life who encourage him to reach beyond the confines of Limerick and do something daring with his life. McCourt presents Frank's decision to leave the safety of a pensioned job at the post office not simply as a product of Frank's bravery, but as the result of the encouragement of these good men.

Frank's decision to leave Limerick does not meet with everyone's approval. By writing of Mrs. O'Connell's anger, McCourt shows us that when one refuses to accept the limits imposed by his poverty, those who *did* accept the limits tend to become resentful.

CHAPTERS XVII–XIX

SUMMARY: CHAPTER XVII

On the eve of his sixteenth birthday, Frank goes to the pub for his first pint. Traditionally, fathers take their sons for the first pint, but because Malachy is gone, Pa Keating takes Frank. The men talk about Hermann Goering's suicide and the horror of the concentration camps. Frank gets very drunk. He leaves the pub and decides he wants to confess his sins before he turns sixteen, but he is sent away from the priests' house because he is drunk. Frank goes home to Angela and picks a fight with her about Laman Griffin, for the first time telling her he knows that she was sleeping with him. Angered, he slaps her. Although he feels sorry for what he has done, Frank reasons that none of this would have happened had Angela not slept with Laman.

The next day, Frank goes to church and wonders angrily why he ever prayed to St. Francis of Assisi, who has not helped him or saved Theresa or prevented children from being murdered in concentration camps. A kind priest named Father Gregory sees Frank crying and says that if he wants to, Frank can talk about what is troubling him. Frank tells him everything; about his dead siblings, his father, having sex with Theresa, hitting his mother, masturbating, and the unfairness of a world in which no one can be punished for what happened at the concentration camps. Father Gregory listens and says that since God has forgiven him, Frank must forgive himself.

Frank begins working for Mr. McCaffrey at Easons Ltd. delivering the Protestant newspaper *The Irish Times*. His coworkers Peter and Eamon spend most of the day running into the bathroom to masturbate over pictures of women in the magazines. One day, the delivery boys have to race around Limerick tearing out a page about contraception from *John O'London's Weekly* magazine, because the government has declared the article unfit for the Irish people to read. Eamon advises Frank to stash some of these pages and then sell them later. Many wealthy people in Limerick approach Frank and ask if he has any copies of the article, and Frank earns nine pounds selling the contraband sheet. He puts eight pounds aside for his fare for America, pays off Peter so he will not tell McCaffrey, and buys his family a big dinner.

Angela has a new job working in the home of an old man named Mr. Sliney, who used to be a friend of Mr. Timoney. One day, Frank has tea with his mother in Mr. Sliney's house, and he meets the wealthy owner. Angela looks contented working in the big, clean, richly appointed house.

Frank becomes the senior boy working for Mr. McCaffrey, and continues to dream about going to America. Frank's brother Malachy works at a rich Catholic private school, but gets fired because he acts happy and confident instead of browbeaten. Malachy moves to England and gets a job in a gas works shoveling coal, and waits to join Frank in America.

SUMMARY: CHAPTER XVIII

> *I'm on deck the dawn we sail into New York. I'm sure I'm in a film. . . . [T]he sun turns everything to gold . . . no one has a care in the world.*
> (See QUOTATIONS, p. 61)

Frank spends three years working at Easons and writing letters for Mrs. Finucane. The old woman dies the night before his nineteenth birthday, and Frank takes seventeen pounds from her purse and forty of the hundred pounds in her trunk upstairs. Feeling like Robin Hood, he throws her ledger into the River Shannon so that no more impoverished debtors will have to pay back the money they owe.

Frank now has enough cash to book passage on a ship to America. He tells Angela he is leaving, and she cries. Frank walks around town, trying to memorize the familiar sights. Now that he is going, there are times that he wants to stay home. Some nights, he sits around the fire with his family, and they all cry at the thought of Frank's departure.

The McCourts throw a party on the night before Frank's departure. Pa Keating and Aunt Aggie attend.

On board his ship, the *Irish Oak,* Frank wishes he had stayed in Ireland, taken the post office exam, and provided for his mother and brothers. As he cries, a priest from Limerick who now lives in Los Angeles approaches and begins talking about how hard it is to leave Ireland. Eventually, the ship reaches Manhattan, which looks to Frank like a vision from a movie. The ship gets rerouted to Albany, New York, and on its way stops in Poughkeepsie. A small boat sails up to the ship, and its Irish pilot invites the First Officer, the priest, and their friends to a party onshore. Frank accompanies the priest, and is taken to a house where he meets a group of flirtatious women. The men pair off with the women; Frank has a drink and ends up having sex with a woman called Frieda. The priest is disapproving. On deck back at the ship, the Wireless Officer says to Frank, "Isn't this a great country altogether?"

SUMMARY: CHAPTER XIX
This chapter consists of one word. In answer to the Wireless Officer's question at the end of Chapter XVIII, "Isn't this a great country altogether?" Frank replies simply, "'Tis."

ANALYSIS: CHAPTERS XVII–XIX
In these final chapters, Frank comes to terms with his religion. He has a moment of painful honesty in front of the statue of St. Francis, when he expresses his anger at the unfairness of life, and the seeming futility of his prayers. He finally expresses anger at the church, but he also finally feels its capacity to heal. McCourt shows us that although the Catholic church may compound the guilt that Frank feels about his bad behavior, it also has the unparalleled power of forgiveness. When Frank goes to Confession and pours out his

worries to the priest, he is forgiven and leaves the church with every burden lifted from his back. He is perfectly happy.

As the book progresses, Frank's formative experiences center less on his family and his mother, and more on his individual process of maturation: he encounters boys who feel no shame about their own sexual impulses, he learns about birth control, he steals from an old woman and feels perfectly justified, he sleeps with a married woman and feels little but elation. While Frank is still a moral person, some of his childish worry and moral fastidiousness is being replaced by a mature toughness.

Frank leaves for the United States filled with expectation, but he also remains strongly connected to Ireland and committed to providing for his family.

The final chapter ends with a simple statement of agreement. Placing the word "'Tis"—a colloquial contraction for "it is"—in a chapter by itself emphasizes how vehemently Frank agrees that America is a great country. It ends the "epic of woe" with a glimpse of hope.

IMPORTANT QUOTATIONS EXPLAINED

1. When I look back on my childhood I wonder how I
    survived at all. It was, of course, a miserable
    childhood: the happy childhood is hardly worth your
    while. Worse than the ordinary miserable childhood is
    the miserable Irish childhood, and worse yet is the
    miserable Irish Catholic childhood.
        . . . nothing can compare with the Irish version:
    the poverty; the shiftless loquacious alcoholic father;
    the pious defeated mother moaning by the fire;
    pompous priests; bullying schoolmasters; the English
    and the terrible things they did to us for eight hundred
    long years.

This passage introduces McCourt's memoir. It is one of the only
times in the narrative that we hear the adult McCourt expressing a
strong, clear opinion. From this point on, the narration proceeds
from a child's point of view. While we are able to infer implied opinions, the narrator never again expresses his views overtly. Young
Frank simply reports events objectively.

   In this opening passage, the author's wry humor contrasts with
the bleakness of his subject matter: a child with an unhappy family
life who encounters oppressive authoritarians at church and at
school, and who is further demoralized by the historical injustices
done to his country. Throughout the autobiography, the author
reports on his trouble as he does here—with good-natured humor,
and without self-pity.

2. The master says it's a glorious thing to die for the Faith and Dad says it's a glorious thing to die for Ireland and I wonder if there's anyone in the world who would like us to live. My brothers are dead and my sister is dead and I wonder if they died for Ireland or the Faith. Dad says they were too young to die for anything. Mam says it was disease and starvation and him never having a job. Dad says, Och, Angela, puts on his cap and goes for a long walk.

This quotation comes from Chapter IV. McCourt points out the danger of sentimentalizing death. When adults tell children to look forward to death, children will lose motivation and abandon their ambitions. This quotation uses the rhythm and style of a real conversation, which reveals Frank's awareness of his parents' conflicting views. Angela is typically hard-nosed and feisty, blaming the death of her children on Malachy's inability to hold a job and feed his family. Malachy's behavior is also typical, for he often says "och, aye" in response to difficult situations, and then goes out to escape conflict rather than confront or resolve it.

3.   I know when Dad does the bad thing. I know when he
     drinks the dole money and Mam is desperate and has
     to beg . . . but I don't want to back away from him
     and run to Mam. How can I do that when I'm up with
     him early every morning with the whole world asleep?

This quotation comes from Chapter VIII. Throughout the novel,
Frank struggles to reconcile his love for Malachy with his anger at
the way Malachy's drinking nearly destroys the family. As this passage shows, Frank has an enormous amount of respect and love for
his father, and he cherishes the time they spend together. At the
same time, however, Frank realizes that his respect for his father
might offend his mother. When Malachy has been drinking, the rest
of the children refuse to talk to their father. McCourt reveals here
that Malachy's drinking causes not only hunger and monetary ruin
for the family, it forces the children to choose between their mother
and father.

4.   Mam turns toward the dead ashes in the fire and
        sucks at the last bit of goodness in the Woodbine butt
        caught between the brown thumb and the burnt
        middle finger. Michael . . . wants to know if we're
        having fish and chips tonight because he's hungry.
        Mam says, Next week, love, and he goes back out to
        play in the lane.

In Chapter IX, Frank observes his mother's growing despondency
as another week passes without the arrival of a paycheck from
England. The ashes in the fire symbolize the crumbling of Angela's
hopes: her dreams have withered and collapsed, leaving her with
only cigarettes for comfort. Frank considers himself mature in comparison to his younger brother's naïve sanguinity. Frank knows that
the promise of fish and chips is an empty one, because money will
never arrive from their father. He knows that next week they're
likely to face the same hunger, and the same frustrations.

QUOTATIONS

5.   I'm on deck the dawn we sail into New York. I'm sure
      I'm in a film, that it will end and lights will come up in
      the Lyric Cinema. . . . Rich Americans in top hats
      white ties and tails must be going home to bed with
      the gorgeous women with white teeth. The rest are
      going to work in warm comfortable offices and no
      one has a care in the world.

Frank's arrival in America at the conclusion of *Angela's Ashes* is
presented as a dream sequence. The narrator's surreal perceptions
of American life—men dressed in top hats and accompanied by
beautiful women—are more poignant than ridiculous, for they
show how Frank has come to idealize the country of his birth. We
assume that Frank's vision will be tainted once he gets off the boat,
but a few pages later, he actually does go home to bed with a gor-
geous woman, and we begin to have hope that his life in America
will be more successful than even he ever dreamed.

KEY FACTS

FULL TITLE
Angela's Ashes: A Memoir

AUTHOR
Frank McCourt

TYPE OF WORK
Memoir; autobiography

GENRE
Memoir—a type of autobiography in which the author writes a personal record of the events, people, and situations that have shaped his or her life. Memoirs can span an entire lifetime, but often focus on a specific period of the writer's life.

LANGUAGE
English, with use of Irish, English, and American dialects

TIME AND PLACE WRITTEN
Early 1990s, New York

DATE OF FIRST PUBLICATION
September 1996

PUBLISHER
Scribner / Simon and Schuster Inc.

NARRATOR
Frank McCourt

POINT OF VIEW
First person

TONE
Humorous, self-effacing, matter-of-fact. McCourt matches his tone to the age of the narrator, becoming more serious and worldly as the narrative progresses.

TENSE
Present tense or immediate past; the author writes as though he is experiencing events for the first time as they unfold.

SETTING (TIME)
Late 1930s and 1940s

SETTING (PLACE)
Brooklyn, New York (briefly); Limerick, Ireland

PROTAGONIST
Frank McCourt

MAJOR CONFLICT
Frank faces hunger, neglect, his father's alcoholism, oppressive weather, and illness in the face of the broader struggle that defines his memoir—getting out of Ireland and rising up from poverty. Along the way he faces opposition from schoolmasters, priests, family members, and people in all positions of authority who look down on him because of his lower-class status.

RISING ACTION
Frank increasingly condemns his father's irresponsibility but worries also about the morality of his own behavior; he determines to make a success of himself in America.

CLIMAX
Near the end, a priest absolves Frank of all his sins, allowing Frank to leave for America with a clear conscience and to reassert control over his future. At this point, Frank's dream of escaping Ireland and overcoming poverty becomes possible.

FALLING ACTION
Frank earns enough money to leave for America and bids an emotional farewell to Ireland.

THEMES
The limitations imposed by class; hunger

MOTIFS
Guilt; anti-English sentiment; stories, songs, and folktales

SYMBOLS
The River Shannon; eggs; ashes

FORESHADOWING
The death of baby Margaret anticipates Frank's near-continual state of bereavement in Limerick, as he struggles to cope with the loss of two of his brothers, Theresa Carmody, and many other friends and relations.

KEY FACTS

STUDY QUESTIONS & ESSAY TOPICS

STUDY QUESTIONS

1. *Why does Frank rarely blame his father for the suffering that his alcoholism inflicts upon the family? How does this lack of censure affect the moral tone of McCourt's memoir?*

Readers might find surprising the fact that Frank does not outwardly condemn his father for his selfish actions; Malachy drinks away his wages, his dole, and even the money relatives sent for baby Alphie, but McCourt is not interested in airing grievances about his childhood. Rather, he aims to convey the events of his youth as he experienced them. McCourt describes Malachy as he saw him as a child—a father who came home reeling and rousting the boys out of bed, but who also sat with his sons in front of the fire, telling stories and sharing tea. The portrayal leaves us with an impression of a deep fondness, a great love between father and son.

McCourt's memoir lacks the accusatory, resentful tone we might expect. Frank spends more time chastising himself for his own sins—such as masturbating and listening to rude stories—than he does complaining about his father's sins. Once again, this suggests that McCourt's primary aim is to convey the self-conscious emotions he experienced in his youth, rather than to voice judgments he may have formed about his father or other family members later in life. McCourt does not set out to demonize his father's vices and promote his own virtues. Instead, he draws an evenhanded picture that encourages the reader to sympathize with everyone.

2. *What role do women play in McCourt's memoir? Is it fair to describe their characterization as stereotypical?*

The women in McCourt's memoir share certain traits. The older women seem hardened, critical, and embittered. In contrast, the younger women in Frank's memoir, such as Theresa Carmody and Frieda, whom Frank sleeps with on his first night in America, are gregarious and sexually forward. They are free with their bodies and seemingly desperate for male affection.

However, McCourt does not dismiss the women in his life as mere stereotypes. In fact, he paints a subtler and more varied picture of women than might be apparent at first glance. Frank does not have many female friends during his childhood, and the women he meets during his adolescence therefore seem striking and unfamiliar, which might explain their stereotypical depiction. As Frank gets to know these women more closely, his portrayal of them becomes fairer and more authentic. For example, Frank is initially bewildered by Theresa Carmody's forwardness but, as the couple's relationship deepens, he grows to admire Theresa for her courage and to empathize with her need for romantic solace. Theresa is older than Frank, and she knows she will die soon. She is not a sexual predator, as we come to learn, but a brave woman trying to enjoy life while she can.

Grandma, Aunt Aggie, and the McNamara sisters are characterized as ill-tempered and petulant, but again, McCourt describes these women from the limited perspective of his youth. Young Frank does not understand the acute disappointment that these women have encountered in their lives, and he fails to perceive that their gruffness masks underlying affection. As he matures, Frank's understanding of women deepens, and thus his characterization of women grows more complex and sensitive. In particular, he forms a closer relationship with Angela founded on a deeper understanding of her plight. From the beginning, Frank's depiction of his mother is anything but unfair; she is described not as a stereotypical woman, but as a loving and fiercely devoted mother whose flaws are excusable in light of the struggle that she has endured.

3.   *What is Frank's relationship to Catholicism, and does this relationship change as the memoir progresses?*

Some of the most important moments in Frank's childhood revolve around Catholic sacraments such as First Confession, First Communion, and Confirmation. In practice, Frank is a good Catholic: he attends Confession, worries about the sins he has committed, and prays frequently. Frank begins to question his own religious integrity and fixates on his sins. Because Frank becomes increasingly self-critical, he turns to sources of comfort other than faith, such as books, plays, stories, and newspapers, in order to escape from the harshness of reality. After he begins his sexual relationship with Theresa, Frank cannot go to Confession, because he thinks that his sins are unpardonable. Frank never abandons his faith, however, even if he doubts his chances for redemption. Before leaving for America, he confesses his sins to a kindly priest and, for the first time, feels the powerful relief of repentance and forgiveness.

SUGGESTED ESSAY TOPICS

1. In what ways does McCourt use his infancy in New York to foreshadow his experiences in Limerick?

2. What role do Frank's and his friends' escapades play in establishing a sense of fun and vitality within the memoir?

3. What do you think McCourt's primary motivation was for writing his memoir? To earn the sympathy of his readers? To teach them something? Explain.

4. Does Frank's relationship with Ireland change during his childhood? If so, how does this affect his subsequent return to the United States?

REVIEW & RESOURCES

QUIZ

1. Why did Angela and Malachy McCourt marry in New York?

   A. They were in love.
   B. Malachy thought that Angela was rich.
   C. Angela was pregnant.
   D. Both were so drunk that they did not know what they were doing.

2. Why does Angela's family initially view Frank's father with suspicion?

   A. The Sheehans are wary of Malachy's northern ways and "odd" manner.
   B. They think Malachy abuses Angela and is violent toward his children.
   C. Malachy insults them at every opportunity.
   D. It is apparent that Malachy cheats on his wife.

3. When Malachy comes home drunk, what does he tell his sons they must do?

   A. Show respect to their mother
   B. Go out and earn money to pay for his drinking habit
   C. Pray to the Virgin Mary
   D. Die for Ireland

4. Why is Nora Molloy's husband, Peter, famous in Limerick?

   A. He has fits and is an expert on sex.
   B. He is known as the champion pint drinker of Limerick.
   C. He can read backward while standing on his head.
   D. He always buys everyone a drink.

5.   What image strikes Frank when he finds his father in the
     pub on the day of Eugene's funeral?

     A.   The sight of Malachy's pint of black Guinness resting
          on Eugene's white coffin
     B.   His father's ashen face as he drinks his pint
     C.   His mother sobbing outside as his father drinks away
          the money for the burial
     D.   The sight of the barman crying in sympathy over
          Malachy's bereavement

6.   How many families use the public lavatory outside the
     McCourts' home in Roden Lane?

     A.   Just the McCourts
     B.   2 families
     C.   11 families
     D.   50 families

7.   Why does Frank's Grandma fret that she has "God in
     me backyard"?

     A.   Because she is visited by an archangel in the middle of
          the night
     B.   Because Frank tells her that he's seen the Messiah
          standing by the fence
     C.   Because she is delusional
     D.   Because Frank threw up his Communion wafer in
          her backyard

8.   In what way is Grandma's lodger Bill Galvin unusual?

     A.   He does not drink Guinness.
     B.   He is kind to Frank.
     C.   He is a Protestant.
     D.   He advises Malachy to curb his drinking habit.

9. Why does Angela think Frank is rejected from becoming an altar boy?

   A. She ascribes it to class distinction and social prejudice.
   B. She insists that Frank did not know enough Latin.
   C. She thinks Frank is too ugly.
   D. She thinks Malachy's reputation as an alcoholic has blighted Frank's prospects.

10. What elements of his stay in the hospital does Frank enjoy?

   A. The wonderful views from his window
   B. The fact that all the nurses treat him with respect
   C. The opportunity to sleep all day and discuss his problems with Seamus
   D. The clean sheets, good food, and books

11. Why does Angela think that the women in her street have a "low-class" mentality?

   A. They tell everyone how much money their husbands are earning in England
   B. They call out to their children to tell them what they are having for dinner
   C. Angela senses that they dislike her, which makes her defensive and critical
   D. Frank told Angela that he overheard them gossiping about his father

12. After which country do the McCourts nickname their second floor?

   A. Italy
   B. Spain
   C. Portugal
   D. Austria

13. Why does Frank find it difficult to condemn his father for his drinking?

    A.   Frank remembers the cozy mornings he spends with his father in front of the fire.

    B.   Frank realizes that his mother can always beg for more money at the St. Vincent de Paul Society.

    C.   Malachy gives Frank a "Friday Penny" every week, which buys Frank's silence.

    D.   Frank understands that his father needs to drown his sorrows over the deaths of Oliver, Eugene, and Margaret.

14. Why does Mr. Hannon have to retire from his job delivering coal?

    A.   The sores on his legs restrict his movement.

    B.   His horse dies.

    C.   Frank's eyesight deteriorates, and Mr. Hannon decides that he cannot do the job by himself.

    D.   He dies of consumption.

15. How does Frank spend his fourteenth birthday?

    A.   He goes to the movies and buys himself fish and chips.

    B.   Aunt Aggie buys her nephew new clothes for work, and Frank stands by the River Shannon and cries.

    C.   Angela throws Frank a big surprise party to which she invites all of his school friends.

    D.   Frank visits the hospital to read to Mr. Timoney.

16. What is Frank's father's first and only Christmas present to his family?

    A.   New boots and coats for his sons

    B.   A book of Irish folktales

    C.   A turkey for their Christmas dinner

    D.   A half-eaten box of chocolates

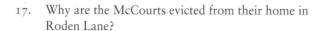

17. Why are the McCourts evicted from their home in Roden Lane?

    A. For insulting the rent collector

    B. For owing four weeks' rent and destroying an internal wall

    C. For not cleaning the public lavatory next to their home

    D. For trying to blackmail their landlord

18. Why does the protagonist leave Laman Griffin's house to stay with Ab Sheehan?

    A. He is repelled by Laman's poor standards of hygiene.

    B. Angela throws Frank out of the house for being disrespectful.

    C. Frank is angry about being cheated out of the use of Laman's bicycle and is also disgusted by the fact that Laman is having sex with his mother.

    D. Michael tells Frank that Laman is stealing money from Angela.

19. Why does Frank not take the post office exam?

    A. He thinks he would fail it.

    B. He arrives late and is not allowed into the exam room.

    C. Frank decides to sacrifice the security of a boring job in order to follow his dreams.

    D. Frank gets fired before he can take the exam.

20. Why does Mr. McCaffrey tell Frank that he can only go up in life?

    A. Because Frank has the right attitude about delivering newspapers

    B. Because Frank always does what he is told

    C. Because Frank is witty and highly intelligent

    D. Because Frank lives in a lane, the lowest standard of residence

REVIEW & RESOURCES

21. What does a priest tell Frank after the protagonist confesses to hitting his mother and damning Theresa Carmody to hell?

    A. He says that Frank is beyond redemption.
    B. He says that God will overlook his sins if Frank gives money to the Catholic church.
    C. He states that God forgives him and so Frank must forgive himself.
    D. The priest asserts that no one is perfect and that Frank's sins do not matter.

22. What is printed on the page that Frank is ordered to tear from all copies of the magazine *John O' London's Weekly*?

    A. An article on contraception
    B. An article on abortion
    C. A picture of a woman in sexy underwear
    D. An article on euthanasia

23. What does Frank do with Mrs. Finucane's ledger of debts after his employer dies?

    A. He hands it over to the police
    B. He throws it in the trash
    C. He takes it with him to America as a personal discouragement to becoming greedy
    D. He throws it into the River Shannon

24. What does Frank observe on his last night in Limerick?

    A. A lunar eclipse
    B. A shooting star
    C. A massive fireworks display celebrating his departure
    D. A UFO

25. To what does Frank compare his arrival in New York?

    A. A Shakespearean drama
    B. A movie
    C. An opera by Wagner
    D. A dream

SUGGESTIONS FOR FURTHER READING

DOYLE, RODDY. *Paddy Clark, Ha Ha Ha*. New York: Viking Penguin, 1994.

MCCOURT, FRANK. *'Tis*. New York: Simon and Schuster Trade, 2000.

MCCOURT, MALACHY. *A Monk Swimming: A Memoir*. New York: Hyperion, 1998.

————. *Singing My Him Song*. New York: HarperCollins, 2000.

SPARKNOTES
TEST PREPARATION
GUIDES

The SparkNotes team figured it was time to cut standardized tests down to size. We've studied the tests for you, so that SparkNotes test prep guides are:

Smarter:
Packed with critical-thinking skills and test-
taking strategies that will improve your score.

Better:
Fully up to date, covering all new features of the tests,
with study tips on every type of question.

Faster:
Our books cover exactly what you need to
know for the test. No more, no less.

SparkNotes Study Guides: